The Life of Prophet Isa AS & Prophet Muhammad SAW

English Edition

by

Jannah Firdaus Mediapro

2020

Prologue

The Life of Prophet Isa AS & Prophet Muhammad SAW from Islamic Perspective Based from The Noble Quran and Al-Hadith.

In many verses of the Glorious Qur'an Allah SWT (God) the Exalted denied the claim of the Christians that He has a son. A delegation from Nagran came to the Prophet Muhammad SAW. They began to talk about their claim about the Trinity, which is that Allah is three in one, the Father, the Son, and the Holy Spirit, with some disagreement among their sects. That is why Allah affirmed in many verses of the Qur'an that Prophet Jesus or Prophet Isa (Pbuh)is a slave of Allah SWT (God), whom He molded in the womb of his mother like any other of His creatures, and that He created him without a father, as He created Prophet Adam (Pbuh) without a father or a mother.

Allah the Almighty said: *Allah chose Adam, Noah, the family of Abraham and the family of Imran above the Alamin (mankind and jinns) (of their times). Offspring, one of theo other, and Allah is All-Hearer, All-Knower.*

Remember when the wife of Imran said: "O my Lord! I have vowed to You what (the child that) is in my womb to be dedicated for Your services (free from all worldly work; to serve Your Place of worship), so accept this, from me. Verily, You are the All-Hearer, the All Knowing."

Then when she delivered her (child Mary), she said: "O my Lord! I have delivered a female child," and Allah knew better what she delivered, - "and the male is not like the female, and I have named her Mary, and I seek refuge with You (Allah) for her and for her offspring from Satan, the outcast."

So her Lord (Allah) accepted her with goodly acceptance. He made her grow in a good manner and put her under the care of Zechariah. Every time he entered Al-Mihrab (a praying place or a private room), he found her supplied with sustenance.

He said: "O Mary! From where have you got this?"

She said: "From Allah. Verily, Allah provides sustenance to whom He wills, without limit." (Ch 3:33-37 Quran)

Allah SWT (God) declared that He had elected Prophet Adam (pbuh) and the elite of his offspring who obey Allah. Then He specified the family of Prophet Abraham (pbuh), which includes the sons of Prophet Ishmael (pbuh), and the family of Imran, the father of Mary (Maryam). Prophet Muhammad SAW was born in Mecca (Makkah), Arabia, on Monday, 12 Rabi' Al-Awal (2 August A.D. 570). His mother, Aminah Bint Wahb, was the daughter of Wahb Ibn Abdu Manaf of the Zahrah family. His father, 'Abdullah, was the son of Abdul Muttalib. His genealogy has been traced to the noble house of Ishmael, the son of Prophet Abraham in about the fortieth descend. Muhammad's father died before his birth.

Before he was six years old his mother died, and the doubly orphaned Muhammad was put under the charge of his grandfather Abdul Muttalib who took the most tender care of him. But the old chief died two years afterwards. On his deathbed he confided to his son Abu Talib the charge of the little orphan.

When Prophet Muhammad SAW was twelve years old, he accompanied his uncle Abu Talib on a mercantile journey to Syria, and they proceeded as far as Busra. The journey lasted for some months. It was at Busra that the Christian monk Bahira met Muhammad. He is related to have said to Abu Talib: 'Return with this boy and guard him against the hatred of the Jews, for a great career awaits your nephew."

After this journey, the youth of Muhammad seems to have been passed uneventfully, but all authorities agree in ascribing to him such correctness of manners and purity of morals as were rare among the people of Mecca. The fair character and the honorable bearing of the unobtrusive youth won the approbation of the citizens of Mecca, and by common consent he received the title of "Al Ameen," or The Faithful.

The Life of Prophet Isa AS

In many verses of the Glorious Qur'an Allah SWT (God) the Exalted denied the claim of the Christians that He has a son. A delegation from Nagran came to the Prophet Muhammad SAW. They began to talk about their claim about the Trinity, which is that Allah is three in one, the Father, the Son, and the Holy Spirit, with some disagreement among their sects. That is why Allah affirmed in many verses of the Qur'an that Prophet Jesus (Pbuh) is a slave of Allah, whom He molded in the womb of his mother like any other of His creatures, and that He created him without a father, as He created Prophet Adam (Pbuh) without a father or a mother.

Allah the Almighty said: *Allah chose Adam, Noah, the family of Abraham and the family of Imran above the Alamin (mankind and jinns)(of their times). Offspring, one of theo other, and Allah is All-Hearer, All-Knower.*

Remember when the wife of Imran said: "O my Lord! I have vowed to You what (the child that) is in my womb to be dedicated for Your services (free from all worldly work; to serve Your Place of worship), so accept this, from me. Verily, You are the All-Hearer, the All Knowing."

Then when she delivered her (child Mary), she said: "O my Lord! I have delivered a female child," and Allah knew better what she delivered, - "and the male is not like the female, and I have named her Mary, and I seek refuge with You (Allah) for her and for her offspring from Satan, the outcast."

So her Lord (Allah) accepted her with goodly acceptance. He made her grow in a good manner and put her under the care of Zechariah. Every time he entered Al-Mihrab (a praying place or a private room), he found her supplied with sustenance.

He said: "O Mary! From where have you got this?"

She said: "From Allah. Verily, Allah provides sustenance to whom He wills, without limit." (Ch 3:33-37 Quran)

Allah declared that He had elected Adam (pbuh) and the elite of his offspring who obey Allah. Then He specified the family of Abraham (pbuh), which includes the sons of Ishmael (pbuh), and the family of Imran, the father of Mary.

Muhammad Ibn Ishaaq stated that he was Imran Ibn Bashim, Ibn Amun, Ibn Misha, Ibn Hosqia, Ibn Ahriq, Ibn Mutham, Ibn Azazia, Ibn Amisa, Ibn Yamish, Ibn Ahrihu, Ibn Yazem, Ibn Yahfashat, Ibn Eisha, Ibn Iyam, Ibn Rahba am, Ibn David (Dawud).

Prophet Zakariyah's (pbuh) wife's sister had a daughter named Hannah. She was married to Imran, a leader of the Israelites. For many years, the couple remained childless. Whenever Hannah saw another woman with a child, her longing for a baby increased. Although years had passed, she never lost hope. She believed that one day Allah would bless her with a child, on whom she would shower all her motherly love.

She turned to the Lord of the heavens and the earth and pleaded with Him for a child. She would offer the child in the service of Allah's house, in the temple of Jerusalem. Allah granted her request. When she learned that she was pregnant, she was the happiest woman alive, and thanked Allah for His gift. Her overjoyed husband Imran also thanked Allah for His mercy.

However, while she was pregnant her husband passed away. Hannah wept bitterly. Alas, Imran did not live to see their child for whom they had so longed. She gave birth to a girl, and again turned to Allah in prayer: *"O my Lord, I have delivered a female child," and the male is not like the female, and I have named her Mary, and I seek refuge with You (Allah) for her and her offspring from Satan, the outcast." (Ch 3:36 Quran)*

Hannah had a big problem in reference to her promise to Allah, for females were not accepted into the temple, and she was very worried. Her sister's husband Zakariyah, comforted her, saying that Allah knew best what she had delivered and appreciated fully what she had offered in His service. She wrapped the baby in a shawl and handed it over to the temple elders. As the baby was a girl, the question of her guardianship posed a problem for the elders. This was a child of their late and beloved leader, and everyone was eager to take care of her. Zakariyah said to the elders: "I am the husband of her maternal aunt and her nearest relation in the temple; therefore, I will be more mindful of her than all of you."

As it was their custom to draw lots to solve disagreements, they followed this course. Each one was given a reed to throw into the river. They had agreed that whoever's reed remained afloat would be granted guardianship of the girl. All the reeds sank to the bottom except Zakariyah's. With this sign, they all surrendered to the will of Allah and made him the guardian.

To ensure that no one had access to Mary, Zakariyah built a separate room for her in the temple. As she grew up, she spent her time in devotion to Allah. Zakariyah visited her daily to see to her needs, and so it continued for many years. One day, he was surprised to find fresh fruit, which was out of season in her room. As he was the only person who could enter her room, he asked her how the fruit got there. She replied that these provisions were from Allah, as He gives to whom He wills. Zakariyah understood by this that Allah had raised Mary's status above that of other women.

Thereafter, Zakariyah spent more time with her, teaching and guiding her. Mary grew to be a devotee of Allah, glorifying Him day and night.

Ali Ibn Abi Talib narrated that the Prophet Muhammad (pbuh) said: "The best of the world's women is Mary (in her lifetime), and the best of the world's women is Khadija (in her lifetime)." (Sahih Al-Bukhari)

Abu Musa Al-Ashari also narrated that the Prophet Muhammad (pbuh) said: "May among men attained perfection but among women none attained perfection except Mary the daughter of Imran, and Asiya the wife of Pharaoh, and the superiority of Aisha to other women is like the superiority of Tharid (an Arabic dish) to other meals."

While Mary was praying in her temple, an angel in the form of a man appeared before her. Filled with terror, she tried to flee, praying: *"Verily! I seek refuge with the Most Beneficent (Allah) from you, if you do fear Allah."*

The angel said: "I am only a Messenger from your Lord, (to announce) to you the gift of a righteous son."

She said: "How can I have a son, when no man has touched me, nor am I unchaste?"

He said: "So (it will be), your Lord said: "That is easy for me (Allah): And (We wish) to appoint him as a sign to mankind and a mercy from Us (Allah), and it is a matter (already) decreed, (by Allah).'" (Ch 19:18-21 Quran)

The angel's visit caused Mary great anxiety, which increased as the months went by. How could she face giving birth to a child without having a husband? Later, she felt life kicking inside her. With a heavy heart, she left the temple and went to Nazareth, the city in which she had been born where she settled in a simple farm house to avoid the public.

But fear and anxiety did not leave her. She was from a noble and pious family. Her father had not been an evil man nor was her mother an impure woman. How could she prevent tongues from wagging about her honor?

After some months, she could not bear the mental strain any longer. Burdened with a heavy womb, she left Nazareth, not knowing where to go to be away from this depressing atmosphere.

She had not gone far, when she was overtaken by the pains of childbirth. She saw down against a dry palm tree, and here she gave birth to a son. Looking at her beautiful baby, she was hurt that she had brought him into the world without a father. She exclaimed: "I wish I had died before this happened and had vanished into nothingness!"

Suddenly, she heard a voice nearby: "Grieve not, your Lord has placed a rivulet below, and shake the trunk of this tree, from which ripe dates will fall. So eat and drink and regain the strength you have lost; and be of good cheer, for what you see is the power of Allah,

Who made the dry palm tree regain life, in order to provide food for you." For a while she was comforted by Allah's miracle, for it was a sure sign of her innocence and purity.

She decided to return to the city. However, her fears also returned. What was she going to tell the people? As if sharinhis mother's worry, the baby began to speak: "If you meet any person say: 'I have vowed to fast for The Beneficent and may not speak to any human today.'" With this miracle, Mary felt at ease.

As she had expected, her arrival in the city with a newborn baby in her arms aroused the curiosity of the people. They scolded her: "This is a terrible sin that you have committed." She put her finger to her lips and pointed to the child. They asked: "How can we speak to a newborn baby?" To their total amazement, the child began to speak clearly: "I am Allah's servant. Allah has given me the Book, and has made me a prophet, and has blessed me wherever I may be, and has enjoined on me prayers and alms-giving as long as I live. Allah has made me dutiful towards she who had borne me. He has not made me arrogant nor unblessed. Peace unto me the day I was born, the day I die, and the day I shall be raised alive."

Most of the people realized that the baby was unique, for it Allah wills something, He merely says "Be" and it happens. Of course, there were some who regarded the baby's speech as a strange trick, but at least Mary could now stay in Nazareth without being harassed.

Allah the Exalted revealed: *And mention in the Book (the Qur'an, O Muhammad, the story of) Mary, when she withdrew in seclusion from her family to a place facing east. She placed a screen (to screen herself) from them; then We sent to her Our Ruh (angel Gabriel), and he appeared before her in the form of a man in all respects.*

She said: "Verily! I seek refuge with the Most Beneficent (Allah) from you, if you do fear Allah."

The angel said: "I am only a Messenger from your Lord, (to announce) to you the gift of a righteous son."

She said: "How can I have a son, when no man has touched me, nor am I unchaste?" He said: "So (it will be), your Lord said: "That is easy for Me (Allah): and (We wish) to appoint him as a sign to mankind and a mercy from Us (Allah), and it is a matter (already) decreed, (by Allah)."'

So she conceived him, and she withdrew with him to a far place (Bethlehem valley, about four to six miles from Jerusalem). And the pains of childbirth drove her to the trunk of a palm tree. She said: "Would that I had died before this, and had been forgotten and out of sight!"

Then (the babe "Jesus" or Gabriel) cried unto her from below her, saying: "Grieve not! Your Lord has provided you a water stream under you; and shake the trunk of palm tree towards you, it will let fall fresh ripe dates upon you. So eat and drink and be glad, and if you see any human being, say: 'Verily! I have vowed a fast unto the Most Beneficent (Allah) so I shall not speak to any human being this day.'"

Then she brought him (the baby) to her people, carrying him. They said: "O Mary! Indeed you have brought a thing Fariyya (an unheard mighty thing). O sister (the like) of Aaron (not the brother of Moses, but he was another pious man at the time of Mary)! Your father was not a man who used to commit adultery, nor was your mother an unchaste woman."

Then she pointed to him. They said: "How can we talk to one who is a child in the cradle?"

He (Jesus) said: "Verily! I am a slave of Allah. He has given me the Scripture and made me a Prophet; and He has made me blessed wheresoever I be, and has enjoined me prayer, and Zakat, as long as I live, and dutiful to my mother, and made me not arrogant, unblest. And Salam (peace) be upon me the day I was born, and the day I die, and the day I shall be raised alive!"

Such is Jesus, son of Mary. (It is) a statement of truth, about which they doubt (or dispute). It befits not (the Majesty of) Allah that He should beget a son (this refers to the slander of Christians against Allah, by saying that Jesus is the son of Allah). Glorified (and Exalted be He above all that they associate with Him). When He decrees a thing, He only says to it, "Be!" - and it is.

Jesus said: "And verily Allah is my Lord and your Lord. So worship Him (Alone). That is the Straight Path. (Allah's Religion of Islamic Monotheism which He did ordain for all of His Prophets)."

Then the sects differed (the Christians about Jesus), so woe unto the disbeliveers (those who gave false witness saying that Jesus is the son of Allah) from the meeting of a great Day (the Day of Resurrection, when they will be thrown in the blazing Fire).

How clearly will they (polytheists and disbeliveers in the Oneness of Allah) see and hear, the Day when they will appear before Us! But the Zalimun (polytheists and wrong-doers) today are in plain error. And warn them (O Muhammad) of the Day of grief and regrets, when the case has been decided, while now they are in a state of carelessness and they believe not. (Ch 19:16-39 Quran)

It was said that Joseph the Carpenter was greatly surprised when he knew the story, so he asked Mary: "Can a tree come to grow without a seed?" She said: "Yes, the one which Allah created for the first time." He asked her again: "Is it possible to bear a child without a male partner?" She said: "Yes, Allah, created Adam without male or female!"

It was also said that, while pregnant, Mary went one day to her aunt, who reported that she felt as if she was pregnant. Mary in turn, said that she, too, was feeling as if she was pregnant. Then her aunt said: "I can see what is in my womb prostrating to what is in your womb."

The Jewish priests felt this child Jesus was dangerous, for they felt that the people would turn their worship to Allah the Almighty Alone, displacing the existing Jewish tenets. Consequently, they would lose their authority over the people. Therefore, they kept the miracle of Jesus's speech in infancy as a secret and accused Mary of a great misdeed.

As Jesus (pbuh) grew, the signs of prophethood began to increase. He could tell his friends what kind of supper waited for them at home and what they had hidden and where. When he was twelve years old, he accompanied his mother to Jerusalem. There he wandered into the temple and joined a crowd listening to the lecture of the Rabbis (Jewish priests). The audience were all adults, but he was not afraid to sit with them. After listening intently, he asked questions and expressed his opinion. The learned rabbis were disturbed by the boy's boldness and puzzled by the questions he asked, for they were unable to answer him. They tried to silence him, but he ignored their attempts and continued to express his views. Jesus became so involved in this exchange that he forgot he as expected back home.

In the meantime, his mother went home, thinking that he might have gone back with relatives or friends. When she arrived, she discovered that he was not there, so she returned to the city to look for him. At last she found him in the temple, sitting among the learned, conversing with them. He appeared to be quite at east, as if he had been doing this all his life. Mary got angry with him for causing her worry. He tried to assure her that all the arguing and debating with the learned had made him forgot the time.

Jesus grew up to manhood. It was Sabbath, a day of complete rest: no fire could be lit or extinguished nor could females plait their hair. Moses (pbuh) had commanded that Saturday be dedicated to the worship of Allah. However, the wisdom behind the Sabbath and its spirit had gone, and only the letter remained in the Jews' hearts. Also, they thought that Sabbath was kept in heaven, and that the People of Israel had been chosen by Allah only to observe the Sabbath.

They made a hundred things unlawful on Saturday even self-defense or calling a doctor to save a patient who was in bad condition. This is how their life was branded by such hypocrisy. Although the Pharisees were guardians of the law, they were ready to sell it when their interests were involved so as to obtain personal gains. There was, for example, a rule which prohibited a journey of more than one thousand yards on the Sabbath day. What do we expect of the Pharisees in this case? The day before, they transferred their food and drink from their homes two thousand yards away and erected a temporary house so that from tthey could travel a further thousand yards on the Sabbath day.

Jesus was on his way to the temple. Although it was the Sabbath, he reached out his hand to pick two pieces of fruit to feed a hungry child. This was considered to be a violation of the Sabbath law. He made a fire for the old women to keep themselves warm from the freezing air. Another violation. He went to the temple and looked around. There were twenty thousand Jewish priests registered there who earned their living from the temple. The rooms of he temple were full of them.

Jesus observed that the visitors were much fewer than the priests. Yet the temple was full of sheep and doves which were sold to the people to be offered as sacrifices. Every step in the temple cost the visitor money. They worshipped nothing but money. In the temple, the Pharisees and Sadducees acted as if it were a market place, and these two groups always disagreed on everything. Jesus followed the scene with his eyes and observed that the poor people who could not afford the price of the sheep or dove were swept away like flies by the Pharisees and Saducees. Jesus was astonished. Why did the priests burn a lot of offerings inside the temple, while thousands of poor people were hungry outside it?

On this blessed night, the two noble prophets John (pbuh) and Zakariyah (pbuh) died, killed by the ruling authority. On the same night, the revelation descended upon Jesus (pbuh). Allah the Exalted commanded him to begin his call to the children of

Israel. To Jesus, the life of ease was closed, and the page of worship and struggled was opened.

Like an opposing force, the message of Jesus came to denounce the practices of the Pharisees and to reinforce the Law of Moses. In the face of a materialistic age of luxury and worship of gold, Jesus called his people to a nobler life by word and deed. This exemplary life was the only way out of the wretchedness and diseases of his age. Jesus's call, from the beginning, was marked by its complete uprightness and piety. It appealed to the soul, the inner being, and not be a closed system of rules laid down by society.

Jesus continued inviting the people to Almighty Allah. His call was based on the principle that there is no mediation between the Creator and His creatures. However, Jesus was in conflict with the Jews' superficial interpretation of the Torah. He said that he did not come to abrogate the Torah, but to complete it by going to the spirit of its substance to arrive at its essence.

He made the Jews understand that the Ten Commandments have more value than they imagined. For instance, the fifth commandment does not only prohibit physical killing, but all forms of killing; physical, psychological, or spiritual. And the sixth commandment does not prohibit adultery only in the sense of unlawful physical contact between a man and a woman, but also prohibits all forms of unlawful relations or acts that might lead to adultery. The eye commits adultery when it looks at anything with passion.

Jesus was therefore in confrontation with the materialistic people. He told them to desist from hypocrisy, show and false praise. There was no need to hoard wealth in this life. They should not preoccupy themselves with the goods of this passing world; rather they must preoccupy themselves with the affairs of the coming world because it would be everlasting.

Jesus told them that caring for this world is a sin, not fit for pious worshippers. The disbeliveers care for it because they do not know a better way. As for the believers, they know that their sustenance is with Allah, so they trust in Him and scorn this world.

Jesus continued to invite people to worship the Only Lord, Who is without partner, just as he invited them to purify the heart and soul.

His teaching annoyed the priests, for every word of Jesus was a threat to them and their position, exposing their misdeeds.

The Roman occupiers had, at first, no intention of being involved in this religious discord of the Jews because it was an internal affair, and they saw that this dispute would distract the Jews from the question of the occupation.

However, the priests started to plot against Jesus. They wanted to embarrass him and to prove that he had come to destroy the Mosaic Law. The Mosaic Law provides that an adulteress be stoned to death. They brought him a Jewish adulteress and asked Jesus: "Does not the law stipulate the stoning of the adulteress?" Jesus answered: "Yes." They said: "This woman is an adulteress." Jesus looked at the woman and then at the priests. He knew that they were more sinful than she. They agreed that she should be killed according to Mosaic Law, and they understood that if he was going to apply Mosaic Law, he would be destroying his own rules of forgiveness and mercy.

Jesus understood their plan. He smiled and assented: "Whoever among you is sinless can stone her." His voice rose in the middle of the Temple, making a new law on adultery, for the sinless to judge sin. There was none eligible; no mortal can judge sin, only Allah the Most Merciful.

As Jesus left the temple, the woman followed him. She took out a bottle of perfume from her garments, knelt before his feet and washed them with perfume and tears, and then dried his feet with her hair. Jesus turned to the woman and told her to stand up, adding: "O Lord, forgive her sins." He let the priests understand that those who call people to Almighty Allah are not executioners. His call was based on mercy for the people, the aim of all divine calls.

Jesus continued to pray to Allah for mercy on his people and to teach his people to have mercy on one another and to believe in Allah.

Jesus continued his mission, aided by divine miracles. Some Qur'anic commentators said that Jesus brought four people back from the dead: a friend of his named Al-Azam, an old woman's son, and a woman's only daughter. These three had died during his lifetime. When the Jews saw this they said: "You only resurrect those who have died recently; perhaps they only fainted." They asked him to bring back to life Sam the Ibn Noah.

When he asked them to show him his grave, the people accompanied him there. Jesus invoked Allah the Exalted to bring him back to life and behold, Sam the Ibn Noah came out from the grave gray-haired. Jesus asked: "how did you get gray hair, when there was no aging in your time?" He answered: "O Spirit of Allah, I thought that the Day of Resurrection had come; from the fear of that day my hair turned gray."

Allah the Almighty said: *Remember when Allah will say (on the Day of Resurrection): "O Jesus, son of Mary! Remember My Favor to you and to your mother when I supported you with Ruh-ul-Qudus (Gabriel) so that you spoke to the people in the cradle and in maturity; and when I taught you writing, Al Hikmah (the power of understanding), the Torah and the Gospel; and when you made out of the clay, as it were, the figure of a bird, by My Permission, and you breathed into it, and it became a bird by My*

Permission, and you healed those born blind, and the lepers by My Permission, and when you brought forth the dead by My Permission; and when I restrained the Children of Israel from you (when they resolved to kill you) since you came unto them with clear proofs, and the disbeliveers among them said: 'This is nothing but evident magic.'"

And when I (Allah) put in their hearts of the disciples (of Jesus) to believe in Me and My Messenger, they said: "We believe. And bear witness that we are Muslims." (Ch 5:110-111 Quran)

Almighty Allah also revealed: And He Allah will teach him (Jesus) the Book and Al Hikmah (the Sunna, the faultless speech of the Prophets, wisdom, etc.), (and) the Torah and the Gospel.

And will make him (Jesus) a Messenger to the Children of Israel (saying): "I have come to you with a sign from your Lord, that I design for you out of clay, as it were, the figure of a bird, and breathe into it, and it becomes a bird by Allah's Leave; and I heal him who was born blind, and the leper, and I bring the dead to life by Allah's leave. And I inform you of what you eat, and what you store in your houses. Surely, therein is a sign for you, if you believe. And I have come confirming that which was before me of the Torah, and to make lawful to you part of what was forbidden to you, and I have come to you with proof from your Lord. So fear Allah and obey me.

Truly! Allah is my Lord and your Lord, so worship Him (Alone). This is the Straight Path."

Then when Jesus came to know of their disbelief, he said: "Who will be my helpers in Allah's Cause?" The disciples said: "We are the helpers of Allah; we believe in Allah, and bear witness that we are Muslims (we submit to Allah)."

Our Lord! We believe in what You have sent down, and we follow the Messenger (Jesus); so write us down among those who bear witness (to the truth, La ilaha ill Allah - none has the right to be worshipped but Allah).

And they (disbeliveers) plotted (to kill Jesus), and Allah planned too. And Allah is the Best of the planners. (Ch 3:48-54 Quran)

Jesus continued calling people to Almighty Allah and laying down for them what might be called "the law of the Spirit." Once when standing on a mountain surrounded by his disciples, Jesus saw that those who believed in him were from among the poor, the wretched, an the downtrodden, and their number was small. Some of the miracles which Jesus performed had been requested by his disciples, such as their wish for a "holy table" to be sent down from heaven.

Allah the Exalted said: *Remember when the disciples said: "O Jesus, son of Mary! Can your Lord send down to us a table spread (with food) from heaven?" Jesus said: "Fear Allah, if you are indeed believers." They said: "We wish to eat thereof and to be stronger in Faith and to know that you have indeed told us the truth and that we ourselves be its witnesses."*

Jesus, son of Mary, said: "O Allah, our Lord! Send us from heaven a table spread (with food) that there may be for us - for the first and the last of us - a festival and a sign from You; and provide us sustenance, for You are the best of sustainers." Allah said: "I am going to send it down unto you, but if any of you after that disbelieves, then I will punish him with a torment such as I have not inflicted on anyone among all the Alamin (mankind and jinn)." (Ch 5:112-115 Quran)

It was related that Jesus commanded his disciples to fast for thirty days; at the end of it, they asked Jesus to bring food from heaven to break their fast. Jesus prayed to Allah after his disciples had doubted Allah's power. The great table cam down between two clouds, one above and one below, while the people watched. Jesus said: "O Lord, make it a mercy and not a cause of distress." So it fell between Jesus's hands, covered with a napkin.

Jesus suddenly prostrated and his disciples with him. They sensed a fragrance, which they had never smelled before. Jesus said: "The one who is the most devout and most righteous may uncover the table, that we might eat of it to thank Allah for it." They said: "O Spirit of Allah, you are the most deserving."

Jesus stood up, then performed ablution and prayed before uncovering the table, and behold, there was a roasted fish. The disciples said: "O Spirit of Allah, is this the food of this world or of Paradise?" Jesus said to his disciples: "Did not Allah forbid you to ask questions? It is the divine power of Allah the Almighty Who said: 'Be,' and it was. It is a sign from Almighty Allah warning of great punishment for unbelieving mortals of the world. This is the kernel of the matter."

It is said that thousands of people partook of it, and yet they never exhausted it. A further miracle was that the blind and lepers were cured.

The Day of the Table became one of the holy days for the disciples and followers of Jesus. Later on, the disciples and followers forgot the real essence of the miracles, and so they worshipped Jesus as a god.

Almighty Allah asserted: *And remember when Allah will say (on the Day of Resurrection): "O Jesus, son of Mary! Did you say unto men: 'Worship me and my mother as two gods besides Allah?'" He will say: "Glory be to You! It was not for me to say what I had no right to say. Had I said such a thing, You would surely have known it. You know what is in my inner self though I do not know what is in Yours, truly, You, only You, are the All Knower of all that is hidden and unseen. Never did I say to them aught except what You (Allah) did command me to say: 'Worship Allah, my Lord and your Lord', And I was a witness over them while I dwelt amongst them, but when You took me up, You were the Watcher over them, and You are a Witness to all things. (This is a great admonition and warning to the Christians of the whole world). If you punish them, they are Your slaves, and if You forgive them, Verily You, only You are the All Mighty, the All Wise."*

Allah will say: "This is a Day on which the truthful will profit from their truth: theirs are Gardens under which rivers flow (in Paradise) - they shall abide therein forever. Allah is pleased with them and they with Him. That is the great success (Paradise). To Allah belongs the dominion of the heavens and the earth and all that is therein, and He is Able to do all things." (Ch 5:116-120 Quran)

Jesus went on his mission until vice knew that its throne was threatening to fall. So the forces of evil accused him of magic, infringement of the Mosaic Law, allegiance with the devil; and when they saw that the poor people followed him, they began to scheme against him.

The Sanhedrin, the highest judicial and ecclesiastical council of the Jews, began to meet to plot against Jesus. The plan took a new turn. When the Jews failed to stop Jesus' s call, they decided to kill him. The chief priests held secret meetings to agree on the best way of getting rid of Jesus. While they were in such a meeting, one of the twelve apostles of Jesus, Judas Iscariot, went to them and asked: "What will you give me if I deliver him to you?" Judas bargained with them until they agreed to give him thirty pieces of silver known as shekels. The plot was laid for the capture and murder of Jesus.

It was said that the high priest of the Jews tore his garment at the meeting, claiming that Jesus had denied Judaism. The tearing of clothes at that time was a sign of disgust.

The priests had no authority to pass the death sentence at that time, so they convinced the Roman governor that Jesus was plotting against the security of the Roman Empire and urged him to take immediate action against him. The governor ordered thaJesus be arrested.

According to the Book of Matthew, Jesus was arrested and the council of the high priests passed the death sentence upon him. Then, they began insulting him, spitting on his face and kicking him.

It was the Roman custom for the condemned to be flogged before they were executed. So Pilate, the Roman governor, ordered that Jesus be flogged. The Mosaic Law stipulates forty lashes, but the Roman had no limit, and they were brutal lashes. After that, Jesus was handed to the soldiers for crucifixion. They took off his clothes, and kept them. They put a crown of thorns on his head to mock him. According to custom he carried his cross on his back to increase his suffering.

Finally, they reached a place called Golgotha, meaning the Place of Skulls, outside the walls of Jerusalem. Instead of giving him a cup of wine diluted with scent to help lessen the pain on the cross, the soldiers gave Jesus a cup of vinegar diluted with gall. Then they crucified him and, as a further mockery, two thieves with him. So it is written in the Bible.

But the faith of Islam came with views quite different from that of the extend gospels with regards to both the end of Jesus and his nature.

The Glorious Qur'an affirms that Allah the Exalted did not permit the people of Israel to kill Jesus or crucify him. What happened was that Allah saved him from his enemies and raised him to heaven. They never killed Jesus, they killed someone else.

Allah the Almighty declared: *And because of their saying (in boast), "We killed Messiah Jesus, son of Mary, the Messenger of Allah," but they killed him not, nor crucified him, but the resemblance of Jesus was put over another man (and they killed that man) and those who differ therein are full of doubts. They have no certain knowledge, they follow nothing but conjecture. For surely; they killed him not (Jesus, son of Mary): But Allah raised him (Jesus) up (with his body and soul) unto Himself (and he is in the heavens). And Allah is Ever All Powerful, All Wise.*

And there is none of the people of the Scripture (Jews & Christians), but must believe in him (Jesus, son of Mary, as only a Messenger of Allah, and a human being0, before his (Jesus or a Jew's or a Christian's) death (at the time of the appearance of the angel of death). And on the Day of Resurrection, he (Jesus) will be a witness against them. (Ch 4:157-159 Quran)

Almighty Allah also revealed: And remember when Allah said: "O Jesus! I will take you and raise you to Myself and clear you (of the forged statement that Jesus is Allah's son) of those who disbelieve, and I will make those who follow you (Monotheists, who worship none but Allah) superior to those who disbelieve (in the Oneness of Allah, or disbelieve in some of His Messengers, e.g. Muhammad, Jesus, Moses, etc., or in His Holy Books, e.g. the Torah, the Gospel, the Qur'an) till the Day of Resurrection. Then you will return to Me and I will judge between you in the matters in which you used to dispute." (Ch 3:55 Quran).

<hr>

Almighty Allah refuted the claims of the Jews and the Christians in many verses of the Glorious *Qur'an*.

And hey say: "The Most Beneficent (Allah) has begotten a son (or offspring or children) (as the Jews say: Ezra is the son of Allah, and the Christians say that He has begotten a son (Christ), and the pagan Arabs say that he has begotten daughters (angels, etc.))."

Indeed you have brought forth (said) a terrible evil thing. Whereby the heavens are almost torn, and the earth is split asunder, and the mountains fall in ruins, that they ascribe a son (or offspring or children) to the Most Beneficent (Allah).

But it is not suitable for (the Majesty of) the Most Beneficent (Allah) that He should beget a son (or offspring or children). There is non in the heavens and the earth but comes unto the Most Beneficent (Allah) as a slave. Verily, He knows each one of them, and has counted them a full counting. And everyone of them will come to Him alone on the Day of Resurrection (without any helper, or protector or defender). (Ch 19:88-95 Quran)

Allah the Exalted also declared: Yet, they join the jinns as partners in worship with Allah, though He has created them (the jinns), and they attribute falsely without knowledge sons and daughters to Him. Be He Glorified! And Exalted above (all) that they attribute to Him. He is the Originator of the heavens and the earth. How can He have children when He has no wife? He created all things and He is the All-Knower of everything.

Such is Allah, your Lord! La ilaha illa Huwa (none has the right to be worshipped but He), the Creator of all things. So worship Him (Alone), and He is the Wakil (Trustee, Disposer of affairs, Guardian etc.) over all tings.

No vision can grasp Him, but His Grasp is over all vision. He is the Most Subtle and Courteous, Well-Acquainted with all things. (Ch 6:100-103 Quran)

Almighty Allah commanded: O people of the Scripture (Jews and Christians)! Do not exceed the limits in you religion, nor say of Allah aught but the truth. The Messiah Jesus, son of Mary, was (no more than) a Messenger of Allah and His Word, ("Be" - and he was) which He bestowed on Mary and a spirit (Ruh) created by Him; so believe in Allah and His Messengers. Say not: "Three (trinity)!" Cease! (It is) better for you. For Allah is the only One Ilah (God), Glory be to Him (Far Exalted is He) above having a son. To Him belongs all that is in the heavens and all that is in the earth. And Allah is All Sufficient as a Disposer of affairs.

The Messiah will never be proud to reject to be a slave to Allah, nor the angels who are near (to Allah). And whosoever rejects His worship and is proud, then He will gather them all together unto Himself. So, as for those who believed (in the Oneness of Allah - Islamic Monotheism) and did deeds of righteousness, He will give their (due) rewards, and more out of His Bounty. But as for those who refuse His worship and were proud, He will punish them with a painful torment. And they will not find for themselves besides Allah any protector or helper. (Ch 4:171-173 Quran)

Almighty Allah also declared: And the Jews say: Ezra is the son of Allah, and the Christians say: Messiah is the son of Allah. That is a saying from their mouths. They imitate the saying of the disbeliveers of old.

Allah's Curse be on them, how they are deluded away from the truth!

They (Jews and Christians) took their rabbis and their monks to be their lords besides Allah, (by obeying them in things which they made lawful or unlawful according to their own desires without being ordered by Allah) and (they also took as their lord) Messiah, son of Mary , while they (Jews and Christians) were commanded (in the Torah and the Gospel) to worship none but One Ilah (God- Allah) La ilaha illa Huwa (none has the right to be worshipped but He). Praise and glory be to Him, (far above is He) from having the partners they associate (with Him). (Ch 9:30-32 Quran)

Allah the Almighty also revealed: Now ask them (O Muhammad): "Are there (only) daughters for your Lord and sons for them?" Or did We create the angels females while they were witnesses?

Verily, it is of their falsehood that they (Quraish pagans) say: "Allah has begotten off-spring or children (angels are the daughters of Allah)" And, verily, they are liars!

Has He (then) chosen daughters rather than sons? What is the matter with you? How do you decide? Will you not then remember? Or is there for you a plain authority? Then bring your Book if you are truthful!

And they have invented a kinship between Him and the jinns, but the jinn know well that they have indeed to appear (before Him) (i.e. they will be brought for accounts).

Glorified be Allah! (He is free) from what they attribute unto Him! Except the slaves of Allah, whom He chooses (for His Mercy i.e. true believers of Islamic Monotheism who do not attribute false things unto Allah). (Ch 37:149-160 Quran)

And Almighty Allah declared: Surely, in disbelief are they who say that Allah is the Messiah, son of Mary. Say (O Muhammad): "Who then has the least power against Allah, if He were destroy the Messiah, son of Mary, his mother, and all those who are on the earth together?" And to Allah belongs the dominion of the heavens and the earth, and all that is between them. He creates what He wills. And Allah is Able to do all things.

And (both) the Jews and Christians say; "We are the children of Allah and His loved ones." Say: "Why then does He punish you for your sins?" Nay, you are but human beings, of those He has created, He forgive whom He wills and He punishes whom He wills. And to Allah belongs the dominion of the heavens and the earth and all that is between them, and to Him is the return of all.

O people of the Scripture (Jews and Christians)! Now has come to you Our Messenger (Muhammad) making (things) clear unto you, after a break in (the series of) Messengers, lest you say: "there came unto us no bringer of glad tidings and no warner." But now has come unto you a bringer of glad tidings and a warner. And Allah is Able to do all things. (Ch 5:17-19 Quran)

Allah the Exalted warned: Surely they have disbelieved who say: "Allah is the Messiah (Jesus), son of Mary." But the Messiah (Jesus) said: "O Children of Israel! Worship Allah, my Lord and your Lord." Verily, whosoever sets up partners in worship with Allah, then Allah has forbidden Paradise for him, and the Fire will be his abode. And for the Zalimun (polytheists, and wrong-doers) there are no helpers.

Surely, disbeliveers are those who said: "Allah is the third of the three (in a Trinity)." But there is no Ilah (god) (none who has the right to be worshipped) but One Ilah (God- Allah). And if they cease not from what they say, verily, a painful torment will befall the disbeliveers among them.

Will they not repent to Allah and ask His Forgiveness? For Allah is Oft-Forgiving, Most Merciful.

The Messiah (Jesus), son of Mary, was no more than a Messenger; many were the Messengers that passed away before him. His mother (Mary) was a Siddiqah (she believed in the Words of Allah, and His Books. They both used to eat food, as any other human being, while Allah does not eat). Look how We made the Ayat (proofs, evidences, verses, lessons, signs, revelations, etc.) clear to them, yet look how they are deluded away from the truth. (Ch 5:72-75 Quran)

And Almighty Allah ordered: And say: "All the praises and thanks be to Allah, Who has not begotten a son (nor an offspring), and Who has no partner in His Dominion, nor He is low to have a Wali (helper, protector, or supporter). And magnify Him with all the magnificence, (Allahu-Akbar, Allah is the Most Great)." (Ch 17:111 Quran)

The pagans once asked the Prophet Muhammad (pbuh): "To whom is your Lord related, His original ancestors and His various branches of descendants?" It is also reported that the Jews said: "We worship Ezra, the Son of Allah," and the Christians said: "Jesus is the Son of Allah," and the Magians said: "We worship the sun and the moon," an the Pagans said: "We worship idols."

In response to all of them Allah revealed some of His attributes: Unity, Uniqueness, and other substantives:

Say: (O Muhammad): "He is Allah, the One. Allah As-Samad (The Self- Sufficient Master, Whom all creatures need, He neither eats nor drinks). He begets not, nor was He begotten; and there is none co-equal or comparable unto Him." (Ch 112:1-4 Quran)

The Life of Prophet Muhammad SAW

Prophet Muhammad SAW was born in Mecca (Makkah), Arabia, on Monday, 12 Rabi' Al-Awal (2 August A.D. 570). His mother, Aminah, was the daughter of Wahb Ibn Abdu Manaf of the Zahrah family. His father, 'Abdullah, was the son of Abdul Muttalib. His genealogy has been traced to the noble house of Ishmael, the son of Prophet Abraham in about the fortieth descend. Muhammad's father died before his birth.

Before he was six years old his mother died, and the doubly orphaned Muhammad was put under the charge of his grandfather Abdul Muttalib who took the most tender care of him. But the old chief died two years afterwards. On his deathbed he confided to his son Abu Talib the charge of the little orphan.

When Muhammad was twelve years old, he accompanied his uncle Abu Talib on a mercantile journey to Syria, and they proceeded as far as Busra. The journey lasted for some months. It was at Busra that the Christian monk Bahira met Muhammad. He is related to have said to Abu Talib: 'Return with this boy and guard him against the hatred of the Jews, for a great career awaits your nephew."

After this journey, the youth of Muhammad seems to have been passed uneventfully, but all authorities agree in ascribing to him such correctness of manners and purity of morals as were rare among the people of Mecca. The fair character and the honorable bearing of the unobtrusive youth won the approbation of the citizens of Mecca, and by common consent he received the title of "Al Ameen," The Faithful.

In his early years, Muhammad was not free from the cares of life. He had to watch the flocks of his uncle, who, like the rest of the Bani Hashim, had lost the greater part of his wealth.

From youth to manhood he led an almost solitary life. The lawlessness rife among the Meccans, the sudden outbursts of causeless and bloody quarrels among the tribes frequenting the Fair of Okadh (The Arabian Olympia), and the immorality and skepticism of the Quraish, naturally caused feelings of pity and sorrow in the heart of the sensitive youth. Such scenes of social misery and religious degradation were characteristic of a depraved age.

When Muhammad was twenty five years old, he traveled once more to Syria as a factor of a noble and rich Quraishi widow named Khadijah; and, having proved himself faithful in the commercial interests of that lady, he was soon rewarded with her hand in marriage. This marriage proved fortunate and singularly happy. Khadijah was much the senior of her husband, but in spite of the disparity of age between them, the most tender devotion on both sides existed. This marriage gave him the loving heart of a woman who was ever ready to console him in his despair and to keep alive within him the feeble, flickering flame of hope when no man believed in him and the world appeared gloomy in his eyes.

Until he reached thirty years of age, Muhammad was almost a stranger to the outside world. Since the death of his grandfather, authority in Mecca was divided among the ten senators who constituted the governing body of the Arabian Commonwealth. There was no such accord among them as to ensure the safety of individual rights and property. Though family relations afforded some degree of protection to citizens, yet strangers were frequently exposed to persecution and oppression. In many cases they were robbed, not only of their goods, but even of their wives and daughters. At the instigation of the faithful Muhammad, an old league called the Federation of Fudul, i.e., favors was revived with the object of repressing lawlessness and defending every weak individual - whether Meccan or stranger, free or slave - against any wrong or oppression to which he might be the victim within the territories of Mecca.

When Muhammad reached thirty-five years, he settled by his judgment a grave dispute, which threatened to plunge the whole of Arabia into a fresh series of her oft-recurring wars. In rebuilding the Sacred House of the Ka'ba in A.D. 605, the question arose as to who should have the honor of raising the black stone, the most holy relic of that House, into its proper place. Each tribe claimed that honor. The senior citizen advised the disputants to accept for their arbitrator the first man to enter from a certain gate. The proposal was agreed upon, and the first man who entered the gate was Muhammad "Al-Ameen." His advice satisfied all the contending parties. He ordered the stone to be placed on a piece of cloth and each tribe to share the honor of lifting it up by taking hold of a part of the cloth. The stone was thus deposited in its place, and the rebuilding of the House was completed without further interruption.

It is related that, about this time, a certain Usman, Ibn Huwairith, supported by Byzantine gold, made an attempt to convert the territory of Hijaz into a Roman dependency, but the attempt failed, chiefly through the instrumentality of Muhammad.

These are nearly all the public acts related by historians in which Muhammad took part in the first fifteen years of his marriage to Khadijah. As for his private life he is described to have been ever helpful to the needy and the helpless. His uncle Abu Talib had fallen into distress through his endeavors to maintain the old position of his family. Muhammad, being rather rich at this time by his alliance with Khadijah, tried to discharge part of the debt of gratitude and obligation which he owed to his uncle by undertaking the bringing up and education of his son 'Ali. A year later he adopted 'Akil, another of his uncle's sons.

Khadijah bore Muhammad three sons and four daughters. All the males died in childhood, but in loving 'Ali he found much consolation.

About this time, Muhammad set a good example of kindness, which created a salutary effect upon his people. His wife Khadijah had made him a present of young slave named Zaid Ibn Haritha, who had been brought as a captive to Mecca and sold to Khadijah. When Haritha heard that Muhammad possessed Zaid, he came to Mecca and offered a large sum for his ransom. Whereupon Muhammd said: "Let Zaid come here, and if he chooses to go with you, take him without ransom; but if it be his choice to stay with me, why should I not keep him?' Zaid, being brought into Muhammad's presence, declared that he would stay with his master, who treated him as if he was his only son. Muhammad no sooner heard this than he took Zaid by the hand and led him to the black stone of Ka'ba, where he publicly adopted him as his son, to which the father acquiesced and returned home well satisfied. Henceforward Zaid was called the son of Muhammad.

Muhammd was now approaching his fortieth year, and his mind was ever-engaged in profound contemplation and reflection. Before him lay his country, bleeding and torn by fratricidal wars and intolerable dissension's; his people, sunk in barbarism, addicted to the observation of rites and superstitions, were, with all their desert virtues, lawless and cruel. His two visits to Syria had opened to him a scene of unutterable moral and social desolation, rival creeds and sects tearing each other to pieces, carrying their hatred to the valleys and deserts of Hijaz, and rending the townships of Arabia with their quarrels and bitterness.

For years after his marriage, Muhammad had been accustomed to secluding himself in a cave in Mount Hira, a few miles from Mecca. To this cave he used to go for prayer and meditation, sometimes alone and sometime with his family. There, he often spent the whole nights in deep thought and profound communion with the Unseen yet All-Knowing Allah of the Universe. It was during one of those retirements and in the still hours of the night, when no human sympathy was near, that an angel came to him to tell him that he was the Messenger of Allah sent to reclaim a fallen people to the knowledge and service of their Lord.

Renowned compilers of authentic traditions of Islam agree on the following account of the first revelations received by the Prophet.

Muhammad would seclude himself in the cave of Mount Hira and worship three days and nights. He would, whenever he wished, return to his family at Mecca and then go back again, taking wihim the necessities of life. Thus he continued to return to Khadijah from time to time until one day the revelation came down to him and the Angel Gabriel (Jibreel) appeared to him and said: "Read!" But as Muhammad was illiterate, having never received any instruction in reading or writing, he said to the angel: "I am not a reader." The angel took a hold of him and squeezed him as much as he could bear, and then said again: "Read!" Then Prophet said: "I am not a reader." The Angel again seized the Prophet and squeezed him and said: *"Read! In the Name of Your Lord, Who has created (all that exists), has created a man from a clot (a piece of thick coagulated blood). Read! And your Lord is the Most Generous, Who has taught (the writing) by the pen, has taught man that which he knew not." (Ch 96:1-4 Quran).*

Then the Prophet repeated the words with a trembling heart. He returned to Khadijah from Mount Hira and said: "Wrap me up! Wrap me up!" She wrapped him in a garment until his fear was dispelled. He told Khadijah what had occurred and that he was becoming either a soothsayer or one smitten with madness. She replied: "Allah forbid! He will surely not let such a thing happen, for you speak the truth, you are faithful in trust, you bear the afflictions of the people, you spend in good works what you gain in trade, you are hospitable and you assist your fellow men. Have you seen anything terrible?" Muhammad replied: "Yes," and told her what he had seen. Whereupon, Khadijah said: "Rejoice, O dear husband and be cheerful. He is Whose hands stands Khadijah's life bears witness to the truth of this fact, that you will be the prophet to this people." Then she arose and went to her cousin Waraqa Ibn Naufal, who was old and blind and who knew the Scriptures of the Jews and Christians, and is stated to have translated them into Arabic. When she told him of what she had heard, he cried out: "Holy! Holy! Verily, this is the

Namus (The Holy Spirit) who came to Moses. He will be the prophet of his people. Tell him this and bid him to be brave at heart." When the two men met subsequently in the street, the blind old student of the Jewish and Christian Scriptures spoke of his faith and trust: "I swear by Him in Who hand Waraqa's life is, Allah has chosen you to be the prophet of this people. They will call you a liar, they will persecute you, they will banish you, and they will fight against you. Oh, that I could live to those days. I would fight for these." And he kissed him on the forehead.

The first vision was followed by a considerable period, during which Muhammad suffered much mental depression. The angel spoke to the grieved heart of hope and trust and of the bright future when he would see the people of the earth crowding into the one true faith. His destiny was unfolded to him, when, wrapped in profound meditation, melancholy and sad, he felt himself called by a voice from heaven to arise and preach. *O you (Muhammad) enveloped (in garments)! Arise and warn! And your Lord (Allah) magnify! (Ch 74:1-3 Quran)* He arose and engaged himself in the work to which he was called. Khadijah was the first to accept his mission. She was to believe in the revelations, to abandon the idolatry of her people and to join him in purity of heart and in offering up prayers to Allah the Almighty.

At the beginning of his mission, Muhammad - hereinafter called the Prophet - opened his soul only to those who were attached to him and tried to free them from the gross practices of their forefathers. After Khadijah, his cousin' Ali was the next companion. The Prophet used often to go into the desert around Mecca with his wife and young cousin that they might together offer their heart felt thanks to the Lord of all nations for His manifold blessings. Once they were surprised by Abu Talib, the father of 'Ali. He said to the Prophet: "O son of my brother, what is this religion you are following?" "It is the religion of Allah of His Angels, of His Messengers and of our ancestor Abraham," answered the Prophet. "Allah has sent me to His servants, to direct them towards the truth, and you, O my uncle, are the most worthy of all. It is meet that I should thus call upon you and it is meet that you should accept the truth and help in spreading it."

Abu Talib replied: "Son of my brother, I cannot abjure the religion of my fathers; but by the Supreme Lord, while I am alive, none shall dare to injure you." Then turning towards 'Ali, the venerable chief asked what religion was his. Ali answered: "O father, I believe in Allah and His Prophet and go with him." Abu Talib replied: "Well my son, he will not call you to anything except what is good, therefore you are free to go with him."

After 'Ali, Muhammad's adopted son Zaid became a convert to the new faith. He was followed by Abu Bakr, a leading member of the Quraish tribe and an honest, wealthy merchant who enjoyed great consideration among his compatriots. He was but two years younger than the Prophet. His adoption of the new faith was of great moral effect. Soon after, five notables presented themselves before the Prophet and accepted Islam. Several converts also came from lower classes of the Arabs to adopt the new religion.

For three weary long years, the Prophet labored very quietly to deliver his people from the worship of idols. Polytheism was deeply rooted among the people. It offered attractions, which the new faith in its purity did not possess. The Quraish had personal material interests in the old worship, and their prestige was dependent upon its maintenance. The Prophet had to contend with the idolatrous worship of its followers and to oppose the ruling oligarchy, which governed its destinies.

After three years of constant but quiet struggle, only thirty followers were secured. An important change now occurred in the relations of the Prophet with the citizens of Mecca. His compatriots had begun to doubt his sanity, thinking him crazy or possessed by an evil spirit. Hitherto he preached quietly and unobtrusively. He now decided to appeal publicly to the Meccans, requesting them to abandon their idolatry. For this he arranged a gathering on a neighboring hill and there spoke to them of their folly in the sight of Allah in worshipping pieces of stone which they called their gods. He invited them to abandon their old impious worship and adopt the faith of love, truth and purity. He warned them of the fate that had overtaken past races who had not heeded the preaching of former prophets. But the gathering departed without listening to the warning given them by the Prophet.

Having thus failed to induce his fellow citizens to listen to him, he turned his attention to the strangers arriving in the city on commerce or pilgrimage. But the Quraish made attempts to frustrate his efforts. They hastened themselves to meet the strangers first on different routes, to warn them against holding any communication with the Prophet, whom they represented as a dangerous magician. When the pilgrims or traders returned to their homes, they carried with them the news of the advent of the bold preacher who was inviting the Arabs loudly - at the risk of his own life - to abandon the worship of their dear idols.

Now the Prophet and his followers became subject to some persecution and indignity. The hostile Quraish prevented the Prophet from offering his prayers at the Sacred House of the Ka'ba; they pursued him wherever he went; they covered him and his disciples with dirt and filth when engaged in their devotions; they scattered thorns in the places which he frequented for devotion and meditation. Amidst all these trials the Prophet did not waver. He was full of confidence in his mission, even when on several occasions he was put in imminent danger of losing his life.

At this time Hamza, the youngest son of Abdul Muttalib, adopted Islam. Hamza was a man of distinguished bravery, an intrepid warrior, generous and true, whose heroism earned for him the title of the "Lion of Allah." He became a devoted adherent of Islam and everlost his life in the cause.

The Prophet continued preaching to the Arabs in a most gentle and reasonable manner. He called thepeople, so accustomed to iniquity and wrong doings, to abandon their abominations. In burning words which excited the hearts of his hearers, he warned them of the punishment which Allah had inflicted upon the ancient tribes of 'Ad and Thamud who had obstinately disobeyed the teachings of Allah's messengers to them. He adjured them by the wonderful sights of nature, by the noon day brightness, by the night when it spreads its veil, by the day when it appears in glory to listen to his warning before a similar destruction befell them. He spoke to them of the Day of Reckoning, when their deeds in this world will be weighed before the Eternal Judge, when the children who had been buried alive will be asked for what crime they were put to death.

Almighty Allah said: *Nay, they wonder that there has come to them a Warner (Muhammad) from among themselves. So the disbeliveers say: "This is a strange thing! When we are dead and have become dust (shall we be resurrected)? That is a far return." We know that which the earth takes of them (their dead bodies), and with Us is a Book preserved (i.e., the Book of Decrees).*

Nay, but, they have denied the truth (this Qur'an) when it has come to them, so they are in a confused state (can not differentiate between right and wrong). Have they not looked at the heaven above them, how We have made it and adorned it, and there are no rifts in it? And the earth! We have spread it out, and set thereon mountains standing firm, and have produced therein every kind of lovely growth (plants).

An insight and a reminder for every slave turning to Allah (i.e., the one who believes in Allah and performs deeds of His obedience, and always begs His pardon). And We send down blessed water (rain) from the sky, then we produce therewith gardens and grain (every kind of harvests that are reaped). And tall date palms, with ranged clusters; a provision for (Allah's) slaves. And We give life therewith to a dead land. Thus will be the resurrection (of the dead). Denied before them (i.e. these pagans of Makka who denied you, O Muhammad) the people of Noah, and the dwellers of Rass, and the Thamud, and 'Ad, and Pharaoh, and the brethren of Lot, and the dwellers of the Wood, and the people of Tubba, everyone of them denied their Messengers, so My Threat took effect." *(Ch 50: 2-14 Quran)*

Almighty Allah also declared: *All praises and thanks be to Allah Who Alone created the heavens and the earth, and originated the darkness and the light, yet those who disbelieve hold others as equal with their*

Lord. He it is Who has created you from clay, and then has decreed a stated term (for you to die). And there is with Him another determined term (for you to be resurrected), yet you doubt (in the Resurrection).

And He is Allah (to be worshipped Alone) in the heavens and on the earth, He knows what you conceal and what you reveal, and He knows what you earn (good or bad). And never an Ayah (sign) comes to them from the Ayat (proofs, evidences, lessons, signs, revelations, etc.) of their Lord, but that they have been turning away from it.

Indeed, they rejected the truth (The Qur'an and Muhammad) when it came to them, but there will come to them the news of that (the torment) which they used to mock at. Have they not seen how many a generation before them We have destroyed whom We had established on the earth such as We have not established you? And We poured out on them rain from the sky in abundance, and made the rivers flow under them. Yet We destroyed them for their sins, and created after them other generations." (Ch 6:1-6 Quran)

As the number of believers increased and the cause of the Prophet was strengthened by the conversions of many powerful citizens, the Prophet's preaching alarmed the Quraish. Their power and prestige were at stake. They were the custodians of the idols, which the Prophet had threatened to destroy; they were the ministers of the worship, which he denounced; in fact their existence and living wholly depended upon the maintenance of the old institutions. The Prophet taught that in the sight of his Lord all human were equal, the only distinction recognized among them being the weight of their piety.

Allah the Exalted said: *O mankind! We have created you from a male and a female, and made you into nations and tribes, that you may know one another. Verily, the most honorable of you in the Sight of Allah is that believer who has At Taqwa (one of the Muttaqun, pious and righteous persons who fear Allah much, abstain from all kinds of sins and evil deeds which He has forbidden), and love Allah much (perform all kinds of good deeds which He has ordained. Verily! Allah is All-Knowing, All-Aware."* (Ch 49:13 Quran).

The Quraish would have none of this leveling of distinctions, as it reflected upon their long inherited privileges. Accordingly, they organized a system of persecution in order to suppress the movement before it became firmly established. They decided that each family should take upon itself the task of stamping out the new faith on the spot. Each household tortured its own members or adherents or slaves who were supposed to have connected themselves with the new religion. With the exception of the Prophet, who was protected by Abu Talib and his kinsmen, and Abu Bakr, and a few others who were either distinguished by their rank or possessed some influence among the Quraish, all other converts were subjected to different sorts of torture. Some of them were thrown into prison, starved, and then flogged. The hill of Ramada and the place called Bata thus became scenes of cruel torture.

One day the Quraish tried to induce the Prophet to discontinue his teachings of the new religion, which had sown discord among their people. 'Utba Ibn Rabi'a, was delegated to see the Prophet and speak to him. 'Utba said: "O son of my brother, you are distinguished by your qualities; yet you have sown discord among our people and cast dissension in our families; you denounced our gods and goddesses and you charge our ancestors with impiety. Now we are come to make a proposition to you, and I ask you to think well before you reject it." "I am listening to you, O father of Walid," said the Prophet. "O son of my brother, if by this affair you intend to acquire riches, honors, and dignity, we are willing to collect for you a fortune larger than is possessed by any one of us; we shall make you our chief and will do nothing without you. If you desire dominion, we shall make you our king; and if the demon which possesses you cannot be subdued, we will bring you doctors and give them riches until they cure you." When 'Utba had finished his discourse, the Prophet said: "Now listen to me, O father of Walid." "I listen." He replied. The Prophet, recited to him the first thirteen verses of Surah Fussilat, which maybe interpreted as follows: *In the Name of Allah The Most Beneficent, The Most Merciful.*

Ha Mim (These letters are one of the miracles of the Quran, and none but Allah Alone knows their meanings). A revelation from Allah the Most Beneficent, the Most Merciful. A Book whereof the Verses are explained in detail; - a Quran in Arabic for people who know. Giving glad tidings (of Paradise to the one who believes in the Oneness of Allah, Islamic Monotheism) and fears Allah much (abstains from all kinds of sins and evil deeds) and loves Allah much (performing all kinds of good deeds which He has ordained), and warning (of punishment in the Hellfire to be the one who disbelieves in the Oneness of Allah), but most of them turn away, so they listen not.

And they say: "Our hearts are under coverings (screened) from that to which you invite us, and in our ears is deafness, and between us and you is a screen, so work you (on your way); verily we are working (on our way).

Say (O Muhammad): "I am only a human being like you. It is inspired in me that your Ilah (God) is One Ilah (God - Allah), therefore take the Straight Path to Him (with true Faith - Islamic Monotheism) and obedience to Him, and seek forgiveness of Him. And woe to Al-Mushrikeen; (polytheists, pagans, idolaters, and disbeliveers in the Oneness of Allah, etc, those who worship others along with or set up rivals or partners to Allah etc.) Those who give not the Zakat and they are disbeliveers in the Hereafter. Truly, those who believe (in the Oneness of Allah and in His

Messenger Muhammad - Islamic Monotheism) and do righteous good deeds for them will be an endless reward that will never stop (Paradise).

Say (O Muhammad): "Do you verily disbelieve in Him Who created the earth in two Days and you set up rivals (in worship) with Him? That is the Lord of the Alamin (mankind, jinn and all that exists).

He placed therein (the earth) firm mountains from above it, and He blessed it, and measured therein its sustenance (for its dwellers) in four Days equal (all these four days were equal in the length of time), for all those who ask (about its creation). Then He Istawa (rose over) towards the heaven when it was smoke, and said to it and to the earth: "Come both of you willingly or unwillingly." They both said: "We come, willingly." Then He completed and finished from their creation as seven heavens in two days and he made in each heaven with lamps (stars) to b e an adornment as well as to guard (from the devils by using them as missiles against the devils). Such is the Decree of Him the All Mighty, The All Knower.

But if they turn away, then say (O Muhammad): "I have warned you of a Sa'iqa (a destruction awful cry, torment, hit, a thunder bolt) like the Sa'iqa which overtook 'Ad and Thamud (people)." (Ch 41:1-13 Quran).

When the Prophet had finished his recitation, he said to 'Utba: "This is my reply to your proposition; now take what course you find best."

Persecution by the Quraish grew fiercer every day and the sufferings of the Prophet's disciples became unbearable. He had heard of the righteousness, tolerance, and hospitality of the neighboring Christian king of Abyssinia. He recommended such of his companions who were without protection to seek refuge in the kingdom of that pious king, Al Najashi (Negus). Some fifteen of the unprotected adherents of Islam promptly availed themselves of the advice and sailed to Abyssinia. Here they met with a very kind reception from the Negus. This is called the first hijrah (migration) in the history of Islam and occurred in the fifth year of the Prophet Muhammad's mission, A.D. 615. These emigrants were soon followed by many of their fellow sufferers, until the number reached eighty-three men and eighteen women.

The hostile Quraish, furious at the escape of their victims, sent deputes to the king of Abyssinia to request him to deliver up the refugees, that they might be put to death for adjuring their old religion and embracing a new one. The king summoned the poor fugitives and inquired of them what was the religion, which they had adopted in preference to their old faith. Ja'far, son of Abu Talib and brother of 'Ali, acted as spokesman for the exiles. He spoke thus: "O king, we were plunged in the depth of ignorance and barbarism, we adored idols, we lived in unchastity, and we ate dead bodies, and we spoke abomination, we disregarded every feeling of humanity and sense of duty towards our neighbors, and we knew no law but that of the strong, when Allah raised among us a man, of whose birth, truthfulness, honesty, and purity we were aware. He called us to profess the Unity of Allah and taught us to associate nothing with Him; he forbade us the worship of idols and enjoined us to speak the truth, to be faithful to our trusts, to be merciful, and to regard the rights of neighbors; he forbade us to speak evil of the worship of Allah and not to return to the worship of idols of woos and stone and to abstain from evil, to offer prayers, to give alms, to observe the fast. We have believed in him, we have accepted his teachings and his injunctions to worship Allah alone and to associate nothing with Him. Hence our people have persecuted us, trying to make us forego the worship of Allah and return to the worship of idols of wood and stone and other abominations. They have tortured us and injured us until, finding no safety among them, we have come to your kingdom trusting you will give us protection against their persecution."

After hearing the above speech, the hospitable king ordered the deputies to return to their people in safety and not to interfere with their fugitives. Thus the emigrants passed the period of exile in peace and comfort.

While the followers of the Prophet sought safety in foreign lands against the persecution of their people, he continued his warnings to the Quraish more strenuously than ever. Again they came to him with offers of riches and honor, which he firmly and utterly refused. But they mocked at him and urged him for miracles to prove his mission. He used to answer: "Allah has not sent me to work wonders; He has sent me to preach to you."

Thus disclaiming all power of wonder working, the Prophet ever rested the truth of his divine mission upon his wise teachings. He addressed himself to the inner consciousness of man, to his common sense and to his own better judgement. *Say (O Muhammad): "I am only a human being like you. It is inspired in me that your Ilah (God) is One Ilah (God- Allah), therefore take the Straight Path to Him (with true Faith - Islamic Monotheism) and obedience to Him and seek forgiveness of Him. And woe to Al Mushrikeen; (polytheists, pagans, idolaters, and disbeliveers in the Oneness of Allah etc., those who worship others along with Allah or set up rivals or partners to Allah etc. (Ch 41:6 Quran)*

Despite all the exhortation of the Prophet, the Quraish persisted in asking him for a sign. They insisted that unless some sign be sent down to him from his Lord, they would not believe. The disbeliveers used to ask: "Why has Muhammad not been sent with miracles like previous prophets?" T he Prophet replied: "Because miracles had proved inadequate to convince. Noah was sent with signs, and with what effect? Where was the lost tribe of Thamud? They had refused to receive the preaching of the Prophet Salih, unless he showed them a sign and caused the rock to bring forth a living camel. He did what they asked. In scorn they cut the camel's feet and then daring the prophet to fulfill his threats of judgment, were found dead in their beds the next morning, stricken by the angel of the Lord."

There are some seventeen places in the Quran, in which the Prophet Muhammad is challenged to work a sign, and he answered them all to the same or similar effect: Allah has the power of working miracles, and has not been believed; there were greater miracles in nature than any which could be wrought outside of it; and the Quran itself was a great, everlasting miracle. The Quran, the Prophet used to assert to the disbeliveers, is a book of blessings which is a warning for the whole world; it is a complete guidance and explains everything necessary; it is a reminder of what is imprinted on human nature and is free from every discrepancy and from error and falsehood. It is a book of true guidance and a light to all.

As to the sacred idols, so much honored and esteemed by the pagan Arabs, the Prophet openly recited: *They are but names which you have named - you and your fathers - for which Allah has sent down no authority. (CH 53:23 Quran)*

When the Prophet thus spoke reproachfully of the sacred gods of the Quraish, the latter redoubled their persecution. But the Prophet, nevertheless, continued his preaching undaunted but the hostility of his enemies or by their bitter persecution of him. And despite all opposition and increased persecution, the new faith gained ground. The national fair at Okadh near Mecca attracted many desert Bedouins and trading citizen of distant towns. These listened to the teachings of the Prophet, to his admonitions, and to his denunciations of their sacred idols and of their superstitions. They carried back all that they had heard to their distant homes, and thus the advent of the Prophet was made know to almost all parts of the peninsula.

The Meccans, however, were more than ever furious at the Prophet's increasing preaching against their religion. They asked his uncle Abu Talib to stop him, but he could not do anything. At , as the Prophet persisted in his ardent denunciations against their ungodliness and impiety, they turned him out from the Ka'ba where he used to sit and preach, and subsequently went in a body to Abu Talib. They urged the venerable chief to prevent his nephew from abusing their gods any longer or uttering any ill words against their ancestors. They warned Abu Talib that if he would not do that, he would be excluded from the communion of his people and driven to side with Muhammad; the matter would then be settled by fight until one of the two parties were exterminated.

Abu Talib neither wished to separate himself from his people, nor forsake his nephew for the idolaters to revenge themselves upon. He spoke to the Prophet very softly and begged him to abandon his affair. To this suggestion the Prophet firmly replied: "O my uncle, if they placed the sun in my right hand and the moon in my left hand to cause me to renounce my task, verily I would not desist therefrom until Allah made manifest His cause or I perished in the attempt." The Prophet, overcome by the thought that his uncle and protector was willing to desert him, turned to depart. But Abu Talib called him loudly to come back, and he came. "Say whatever you please; for by the Lord I shall not desert you ever."

The Quraish again attempted in vain to cause Abu Talib to abandon his nephew. The venerable chief declared his intention to protect his nephew against any menace or violence. He appealed to the sense of honor of the two families of the Bani Hashim and the Bani Muttalib, both families being kinsmen of the Prophet, to protect their member from falling a victim to the hatred of rival parties. All the members of the two families nobly responded to the appeal of Abu Talib except Abu Lahab, one of the Prophet's uncles, who took part with the persecutors.

During this period, 'Umar Al-Khattab adopted Islam. In him the new faith gained a valuable adherent and an important factor in the future development and propagation of Islam. Hitherto he had been a violent opposer of the Prophet and a bitter enemy of Islam. His conversion is said to have been worked by the miraculous effect on his mind of a Surah of the Quran which his sister was reading in her house, where he had gone with the intention of killing her for adopting Islam. Thus the party of the Prophet had been strengthened by the conversation by his uncle Hamza, a man of great valor and merit; and of Abu Bakr and 'Umar, both men of great energy and reputation. The Muslims now ventured to perform their devotions in public.

Alarmed at the bold part which the Prophet and his followers were not able to assume, and roused by the return of the deputies from Abyssinia and the announcement of their unsuccessful mission, the Quraish determined to check by a decisive blow any further progress of Islam. Towards this end, in the seventh year of the mission, they made a solemn covenant against the descendants of Hashim and Muttalib, engaging themselves to contract no marriage with any of them and to have no communication with them. Upon this, the Quraish became divided into two factions, and the two families of Hashim and Muttalib all repaired to Abu Talib as their chief. Abu Lahab, the Prophet's uncle, however, out of his inveterate hatred of his nephew and his doctrine, went over to the opposite party, whose chief was Abu Sufyan Ibn Harb, of the family of Umayya. The persecuted party, Muslims as well as idolaters betook themselves to a defile on the eastern skirts of Mecca. They lived in this defensive position for three years. The provisions, which they had carried with them, were soon exhausted. Probably they would have entirely perished but for the sympathy and occasional help received from less bigoted compatriots.

Towards the beginning of the tenth year of the mission, reconciliation was concluded between the Quraish and the two families of Hashim and Abdul Muttalib through the intermediation of Hisham, Ibn Umar, and Zobeir, Ibn Abu Umayya. Thus, the alliance against the two families was abolished, and they were able to return to Mecca.

During the period the Prophet and his kinspeople passed in their defensive position, Islam made no progress outside; but in the sacred months, when violence was considered sacrilege, the Prophet used to come out of his temporary prison to preach Islam to the pilgrims. In the following year, both Abu Talib and Khadijah died. Thus the Prophet lost in Abu Talib the kind guardian of his youth who had hitherto protected him against his enemies, and in Khadijah his most encouraging companion. She was ever his angel of hope and consolation. The Prophet, weighed down by the loss of his amiable protector and his beloved wife, without hope of turning the Quraish from idolatry, with a saddened heart, yet full of trust, resolved to exercise his ministry in some of her field. He chose Taif, a town about sixty miles east of Mecca, where he went accompanied by a faithful servant Zaid. The tribe of Thakif, who were the inhabitants of Taif, received Muhammad very coldly. However, he stayed there for one month. Though the more considerate and better sort of men treated him with a little respect, the slaves and common people refused to listen to his teachings; they were outrageously indignant at his invitation to abandon the gods they worshipped with such freedom of morals and lightness of heart. At length they rose against him, and bringing him to the wall of the city, obliged him to depart and return to Mecca.

The repulse greatly discouraged his followers; however, the Prophet boldly continued to preach to the public assemblies at the pilgrimage and gained several new converts, among whom were six of the city of Yahtrib (later called Medina), of the Jewish tribe of Khazraj. When these Yathribites returned home, they spread the news among their people that a prophet had arisen among the Arabs who was to call them to Allah and put an end to their inquiries.

In the twelfth year of his mission, the Prophet made his night journey from Mecca to Jerusalem, and thence to heaven. His journey, known in history as Miraj (Ascension) was a real bodily one and not only a vision. It was at this time that Allah ordered the Muslims to pray the five daily prayers.

Almighty Allah had said: *Glorified (and Exalted) be He (Allah) (above all that evil they associate with Him), Who took His slave Muhammad for a journey by night from AL Masjid al Haram (at Makka) to the farthest mosque (in Jerusalem), the neighborhood whereof We have blessed, order that We might show him (Muhammad) of Our Ayat (proofs, evidences, lessons, signs, etc.). Verily, He is the All Hearer, the All Seer." (Ch 17:1 Quran)*

Abbas Ibn Malik reported that Malik Ibn Sasaa said that Allah's Messenger described to them his Night Journey saying: "While I was lying in Al-Hatim or Al-Hijr, suddenly someone came to me and cut my body open from here to here." I asked Al-Jarud, who was by my side, "What does he mean?" He said: "It means from his throat to his public area," or said, "From the top of the chest." The Prophet further said, "He then took out my heart. Then a gold tray of Belief was brought to me and my heart was washed and was filled (with Belief) and then returned to its original place. Then a white animal which was smaller than a mule and bigger than a donkey was brought to me." (On this Al-Jarud asked: "Was it in the Buraq, O Abu Hamza?" I (Anas) replied in the affirmative. The Prophet said: "The animal's step (was so wide that it) reached the farthest point within the reach of the animals' sight. I was carried on it, and Gabriel set out with me till we reached the nearest heaven.

"When he asked for the gate to be opened, it was asked, 'Who is it?' Gabriel answered, 'Gabriel.' It was asked, 'Who is accompany you?' Gabriel replied, 'Muhammad.' It was asked, 'Has Muhammad been called?' Gabriel replied in the affirmative. Then it was said. 'He is welcomed. What an excellent visit his is!' The gate was opened, and when I went over the first heaven, I saw Adam there. Gabriel said to me: 'This is your father, Adam; pay him your greetings.' So I greeted him and he returned the greetings to me and said: 'You are welcomed, O pious son and pious Prophet.' Then Gabriel ascended with me till we reached the second heaven. Gabriel asked for the gate to be opened. It was asked: 'Who is it?' Gabriel answered: 'Gabriel.' It was asked: 'Who is accompany you?' Gabriel replied, 'Muhammad.' It was asked: 'Has he been called?' Gabriel answered in the affirmative. Then it was said: 'He is welcomed. What an excellent visit his is!' The gate was opened.

"When I went over the second heaven, here I saw John (Yahya) and Jesus (Isa), who were cousins of each other. Gabriel said to me: "These are John and Jesus; pay them your greetings.' So I greeted them and both of them returned my greetings to me and said, 'You are welcomed, O pious brother and pious Prophet.' Then Gabriel ascended with me to the third heaven and asked for its gate to be opened. IT was asked 'Who is it?' And Gabriel replied: 'Gabriel.' It was asked, 'Who is accompany you?' Gabriel replied, 'Muhammad.' It was asked, 'Has he been called?' Gabriel replied in the affirmative. Then it was said: 'He is welcomed, what an excellent visit his is!' The gate was opened, and when I went over the third heaven there I saw Joseph (Yusuf), Gabriel said to me: 'This is Joseph, pay him your greetings.' So I greeted him and he returned the greetings to me and said: 'You are welcomed, O pious brother and pious Prophet.' Then Gabriel ascended with me to the fourth heaven and asked for its gate to be opened. IT was asked 'Who is it?' Gabriel replied, 'Gabriel' It was asked: 'Who is accompany you?' Gabriel replied: 'Muhammad.' It was asked: 'Has he been called?' Gabriel replied in the affirmative. Then it was said: 'He is welcomed, what an excellent visit his is!'

"The gate was opened, and when I went over the fourth heaven, there I saw Enoch (Idris), Gabriel said to me: 'This is Enoch; pay him your greetings.' So I greeted him and he returned the greetings to me and said: 'You are welcomed O pious brother and pious Prophet.' Then Gabriel ascended with me to the fifth heaven and asked for its gate to be opened. It was asked: 'Who is it?' Gabriel replied: 'Gabriel.' It was asked: 'Who is accompany you?' Gabriel replied 'Muhammad.' It was asked: 'Has he been called?' Gabriel replied in the affirmative. Then it was said: 'He is welcomed, what an excellent visit his is!' So when I went over the fifth heaven, there I saw Aaron (Harun), Gabriel said to me: "This is Aaron; pay hyour greetings.' So I greeted him and he returned the greetings to me and said: "You are welcomed, O pious brother and pious Prophet." The Gabriel ascended with me to the sixth heaven and asked for its gate to be opened. It was asked: 'Who is it?' Gabriel replied: 'Gabriel.' It was asked: 'Who is accompanying you?' Gabriel replied: 'Muhammad.' It was said: 'Has he been called?' Gabriel replied in the affirmative. It was said: 'He is welcomed. What an excellent visit his is!'

"When I went over the sixth heaven, there I saw Moses (Musa). Gabriel said to me: "This is Moses; pay him your greeting. So I greeted him and he returned the greetings to me and said: "You are welcomed, O pious brother and pious Prophet." When I left him (Moses) he wept. Someone asked him: 'What makes you weep?' Moses said: 'I weep because after me there has been sent (as Prophet) a young man whose followers will enter Paradise in greater numbers than my followers.' Then Gabriel ascended with me to the seventh heaven and asked for its gate to be opened. It was asked: 'Who is it?' Gabriel replied: 'Gabriel.' It was asked: 'Who is accompanying you?' Gabriel replied: 'Muhammad.' It was asked: 'Has he been called?' Gabriel replied in the affirmative. Then it said: 'He is welcomed. What an excellent visit his is!'

"So when I went (over the seventh heaven), there I saw Abraham (Ibrahim). Gabriel said to me: 'This is your father; pay your greetings to him.' So I greeted him and he returned the greetings to me and said: 'You are welcomed, O pious son and pious Prophet.' Then I was made to ascend to Sidrat-ul-Muntaha (the Lote Tree of the utmost boundary). Behold! Its fruits were like the jars of Hajr (a place near Medina) and its leaves were as big as the ears of elephants. Gabriel said: "This is the Lote Tree of the utmost and boundary.' Behold! There ran four rivers, two were hidden and two were visible, I asked: 'What are these two kinds of rivers, O Gabriel?' He replied: 'As for the hidden rivers, they are two rivers in Paradise and the visible rivers are the Nile and the Euphrates.'

"Then Al-Bait-ul-Ma'mur (the Sacred House) was shown to me and a container full of wine and another full of milk and a third full of honey were brought to me. I took the milk. Gabriel remarked: 'This is the Islamic religion which you and your followers are following.' Then the prayers were enjoined on me: they were fifty prayers a day. When I returned, I passed by Moses, who asked me; 'What have you been ordered to do?' I replied: 'I have been ordered to offer fifty prayers a day.' Moses said: 'Your followers cannot bear fifty prayers a day, and by Allah I have tested people before you, and I have tried my level best with Bani Israel in vain. Go back to your Lord and ask for reduction to lessen your followers'' burden.' So I went back, and Allah reduced ten prayers for me. Then again I came to Moses, but he repeated the same as he had said before. Then again I went back to Allah, and He reduced ten more prayers. When I came to Moses he said the same. I went back to Allah, and He ordered m to observe ten prayers a day. When I came back to Moses, he repeated the same advice, so I went back to Allah and was ordered to observe five prayers a day.

"When I came back to Moses, he said: 'What have you been ordered?' I replied: 'I have been ordered to observe five prayers a day.' He said: 'Your followers cannot bear fear prayers a day, and no doubt, I have got an experience of the people before you, and I have tried my level best with Bani Israel, so go back to your Lord and ask for reduction to lesson your followers' burden.' I said: 'I have requested so much of my Lord that I feel ashamed, but I am satisfied now and surrender to Allah's Order.' When I left, I heard a voice saying: 'I have passed My order and have lessened the burden of My worshippers.'"

In this year, twelve men of Yathrib, of whom ten were of the Jewish tribe of Khazraj and the other two of Aws, came to Meccan and took an oath of fidelity to the Prophet at Al-Aqaba, a hill on the north of that city. This oath was called the Women's' Oath, not that any women were present at this time, but because a man was not thereby obliged to take up arms in defense of the Prophet or his religion, it being the same oath that was afterwards exacted of the women. This oath was as follows: "We will not associate anything with Allah; we will not steal nor commit adultery or fornication, nor kill our children (as the pagan Arabs used to do when they apprehended that they would not be able to maintain them), nor forge calumnies; we will obey the Prophet in everything that is reasonable, and we will be faithful to him in well and sorrow." When they had solemnly engaged to do all this, the Prophet sent one of his disciples, Mus'ab Ibn Umair, home with them to teach them the fundamental doctrines and ceremonies of the religion. Mus'ab, having arrived at Yathrib by the assistance of those who had been formerly converted, gained several new converts, particularly Usaid Ibn Khudair, a chief of man of the city, and Sa'd Ibn Mu'adh, prince of the tribe of Aws. Islam spread so fast that there was a scarce a house that did not have some Muslims in it.

The next year, being the thirteenth of the mission (A.D. 622) Mus'ab returned from Yathrib accompanied by seventy-three men and two women of that city who had adopted Islam, besides others who were as yet unbelievers. On their arrival, these Yathribites immediately sent to the Prophet and invited him to their city. The Prophet was not in great need of such assistance, for his opponents had by this time grown so powerful in Mecca that he could not stay there much longer without imminent danger. He therefore accepted their proposal and met them one night by appointment at Al Aqaba attended by his uncle Al-Abbas, who, though he as not then a convert, wished his nephew well. Al Abbas made a speech to those of Yathrib wherein he told them that, as the Prophet Muhammad was obliged to quit his native city and seek shelter elsewhere, and they had offered him their protection, they would do well not to deceive him; and that if they were not firmly resolved to defend and not to betray him, they had better declare their minds and let him provide for his safety in some other manner. Upon their professing their sincerity, the Prophet swore to be faithful to them, on condition that they should worship none but Allah observe the precepts of Islam, obey the Prophet in all that was right, and protect him against all insults as heartily as they would their wives and families. They then asked him what would be their return, if they should happen to be killed in the cause of Allah; he answered: "Paradise," whereupon they pledged their faith to him and his cause. The Prophet then selected twelve men out of their number to act as his delegates. Thus was concluded the second covenant of Al Aqaba. The Yathribites returned home leaving the Prophet to arrange for the journey to their city. The Prophet directed his followers to seek immediate safety at Yathrib, which they accordingly did. About one hundred families silently disappeared from Mecca and proceeded to Yathrib, where they were received with enthusiasm and much ho spitality. Finally, all the disciples had gone to Yathrib. The Prophet alone remained at Mecca, keeping with him only his young cousin, 'Ali, and his devoted friend Abu Bakr.

The Meccans, fearing the consequence of this new alliance, began to think seriously of preventing Muhammad from escaping to Yathrib. They met in all haste. After several milder expedients had been rejected, they decided that he should be killed. They agreed that one man should be chosen out of every tribe and that each man should strike a blow at him with his sword so that responsibility of the guilt would rest equally on all tribes. The Bani Hashim,

Muhammad's own tribe, were much inferior and therefore would not be able to revenge their kinsman's death.

A number of noble youths were selected for the bloody deed. As the night advanced, the assassins posted themselves round the Prophet's dwelling. They watched all night long, waiting to murder Muhammad when he should leave his house at the early dawn. By some the Prophet had warned of the danger, and he directed 'Ali to lie down in his place and wrap himself up in his green clock, which he did. The Prophet miraculously escaped through the window and he repaired to the house of Abu Bakr, unperceived by door. These, in the meantime, looking through a crevice and seeing 'Ali, whom they mistook for Muhammad himself, asleep, continued watching there until morning. When 'Ali arose, they found themselves deceived. The fury of the Quraish was now unbounded. The news that the would be assassins had returned unsuccessful and that Muhammad had escaped aroused their whole energy. A price of a hundred camels was set upon Muhammad's head.

Narrated 'Aisha Bint Abu Bakr (the wife of the Prophet): "I never remembered my parents believing in any religion other than the true religion (Islam), and (I don't remember) a single day passing without our being visited by Allah's Messenger in the morning and in the evening. When the Muslims were put to test (troubled by the pagans), Abu Bakr set out migrating to the land of Abyssinia (Ethiopia), and when he reached Bark-al-Ghimad, Ibn Ad-Daghina, the chief of the tribe of Qara, met him and said, 'O Abu Bakr! Where are you going?' Abu Bakr replied: 'My people have turned me out (of my country), so I want to wander on the earth and worship my Lord.' Ibn Ad-Dhagina said: 'O Abu Bakr! A man like you should not leave his homeland, nor should he be driven out, because you help the destitute, earn their living, and you keep good relations with your kith and kin, help the weak and the poor, entertain guests generously, and help the calamity-stricken persons. Therefore, I am your protector. Go back and worship your Lord in your town.'

"So Abu Bakr returned and Ibn Ad-Daghina accompanied him. In the evening Ibn Ad-Dhagina visited the nobles of Quraish and said to them. 'A man like Abu Bakr should not leave his homeland, nor should he be driven out. Do you (Quraish) drive out a man who helps the destitute, earns their living, keeps good relations with his kith and kin, helps the weak and poor, entertain guests generously and helps the calamity-stricken persons?' So the people of Quraish could not refuse Ibn Ad-Dhagina's protection, and they said to Ibn Ad-Daghina: 'Let Abu Bakr worship his Lord in his house. He can pray and recite there whatever he likes, but he should not hurt us with it, and should not do it publicly, because we are afraid that he may affect our women and children." Ibn Ad-Dhagina told Abu Bakr all of that. Abu Bakr stayed in that state, worshipping his Lord in his house. He did not pray publicly, nor did he recite Quran outside his house.

"Then a thought occurred to Abu Bakr to build a mosque in front of his house, and there he used to pray and recite the Quran. The women and children of the pagans began to gather around him in great number. They used to wonder at him and look at him. Abu Bakr was a man who used to weep too much, and he could not help weeping or reciting the Quran. That situation scared the nobles of the pagans of Quraish, so they sent for Ibn Ad-Daghina. When he came to them, they said: 'We accepted your protection of Abu Bakr on condition that he should worship his Lord in his house, but he has violated the conditions and he has built a mosque in front of his house where he prays and recites the Quran publicly. We are not afraid that he may affect our women and children unfavorably. So, prevent him from that. If he likes to confine the worship of his Lord to his house, he may do so, but if he insists on doing that openly, ask him to release you from your obligation to protect him, for we dislike to break our pact with you, but we deny Abu Bakr the right to announce his act publicly.' Ibn Ad-Dhagina went to Abu Bakr and said: 'O Abu Bakr! You know well what contract I have made on your behalf; now, you are either to abide by it, or else release me from my obligation of protecting you, because I do not want the Arabs hear that my people have dishonored a contract I have made on behalf of another man.' Abu Bakr replied: 'I release you from your pact to protect me and am pleased with the protection from Allah.' Aisha's narration's continues: "At that time the Prophet was in Mecca, and he said to the Muslims: 'In a dream I have been shown your migration place, a land of date palm trees, between two mountains, the two stony tracts.' So, some people migrated to Medina, and most of those people who had previously migrated to the land of Ethiopia, returned to Medina. Abu Bakr also prepared to leave for Medina, but Allah's Messenger said to him: 'Wait for awhile, because I hope that I will be allowed to migrate also.' Abu Bakr replied: 'Do you indeed expect this? Let my father be sacrificed for you!' The Prophet said: 'Yes.' So Abu Bakr did not migrate for the sake of Allah's Messenger in order to accompany him. He fed two she camels he possessed with the leaves of As-Samur tree that fell on being struck by a stick for four months.

"One day, while we were sitting in Abu Bakr's house at noon, someone said to Abu Bakr: 'This is Allah's Messenger with his head covered coming at a time at which he never used to visit us before.' Abu Bakr said: 'May my parents be sacrificed for him. By Allah he has not come at this hour except for a great necessity.' So Allah's Messenger came and asked permission to enter, and he was allowed to enter. When he entered, he said to Abu Bakr: "Tell everyone who is present with you to go away.' Abu Bakr replied: 'There are none but your family, May my father be sacrificed for you, O Allah's Messenger!'

The Prophet said: 'I have been given permission to migrate.' Abu Bakr said: 'Shall I accompany you? May my father be sacrificed for you, O Allah's Messenger!' Allah's Messenger said: 'Yes.' Abu Bakr said, 'O Allah's Messenger! May my father be sacrificed for you, take one of these two she-camels of mine.' Allah's Messenger replied: 'I will accept it with payment.' So we prepared the baggage quickly and put some journey food in a leather bag for them. Asma, Abu Bakr's daughter, cut a piece from her waist belt and tied the mouth of the leather bag with it, and for that reason she was named 'Dhat-un-Nitaqain' (the owner of two belts).

"Then Allah's Messenger and Abu Bakr reached a cave on the mountain of Thaur and stayed there for three nights. Abdullah Ibn Abi Bakr who was an intelligent and sagacious youth, used to stay with them overnight. He used to leave them before daybreak so that in the morning he would be with Quraish as if he had spent the night in Mecca. He would keep in mind any plot made against them and when it became dark he would go and inform them of it. 'Amir Ibn Fuhaira, the freed slave of Abu Bakr, used to bring the milch sheep (of his master, Abu Bakr) to them a little while after nightfall in order to rest the sheep there. So they always had fresh milk at night, the milk of their sheep, and the milk which they warmed by throwing heated stones in it. 'Amir Ibn Fuhaira would then call the herd away when it was still dark (before daybreak). He did the same in each of those three nights. Allah's Messenger and Abu Bakr had hired a man from the tribe of Bani Ad-Dail from the family of Bani Abd Ibn Adi as an expert guide, and he was in alliance with the family of Al-As Ibn Wail As-Sahmi and he was in the religion of the infidels of Quraish. The Prophet and Abu Bakr trusted him and gave him their two she-camels and took his promise to bring their two she-camels to the cave of the mountain of Thaur in the morning after three nights later. And when they set out, Amir Ibn Futhaira and the guide went along with them and the guide led them, along the seashore." (Sahih Al-Bukhari).

The nephew of Suraqa Ibn Ju'sham said that his father informed him that he heard Suraqa Ibn Jusham saying: "The messengers of the pagans of Quraish came to us declaring that they had assigned for the persons who would kill or arrest Allah's Messenger and Abu Bakr, a reward equal to their bloodmoney. While I was sitting in one of the gatherings of my tribe, Bani Mudlij, a man from them came to us and stood up while we were sitting and said: 'O Suraqa! No , I have just seen some people far away on the seashore, and I think they are Muhammad and his companions.' I, too, realized that it must have been they. But I said: 'No, it is not they, but you have seen so-and-so and so-and-so, whom we saw set out.' I stayed in the gathering for a while and then got up and left for my home, and ordered my slave-girl to get my horse, which was behind a hillock, and keep it ready for me.

"Then I took my spear and left by the back door of my house dragging the lower end of the spear on the ground and keeping it low. Then I reached my horse, mounted it and made it gallop. When I approached them (Muhammad and Abu Bakr), my horse stumbled and I fell down from it. Then I stood up, gold hold of my quiver and took out the divining arrows and drew lots as to whether I should harm them or not, and the lot which I disliked came out. But I remounted my horse and let it gallop, giving no importance to the divining arrows. When I heard the recitation of the Qur'an by Allah's Messenger who did not look hither and thither while Abu Bakr was doing it often, suddenly the forelegs of my horse sank into the ground up to the knees, and I fell down from it. Then I rebuked it, and it got up but could hardly take out its forelegs from the ground, and when it stood up straight again, its forelegs caused dust to rise up in the sky like smoke. Then again I drew lots with the divining arrows, and the lot which I disliked came out. So I called upon them to feel secure. They stopped, and I remounted my horse and went to them. When I saw how I had been hampered from harming them, it came to my mind that the cause of Allah's Messenger (Islam) would become victorious. So I said to them: 'Your people have assigned a reward equal to bloodmoney for your head.' Then I told them all the plans the people of Mecca had made concerning them. Then I offered them some journey food and goods, but they refused to take anything and did not ask for anything, but the Prophet said: 'Do not tell others about us.' Then I requested him to write for me a statement of security and peace. He ordered 'Amir Ibn Fuhaira, who wrote it for me on a parchment, and then Allah's Messenger proceeded on his way." (Sahih Al-Bukhari)

"Narrated 'Urwa Ibn Az-Zubair: "Allah's Messenger met Az Zubair in a caravan of Muslim merchants who were returning from Sham. Az -Zubair provided Allah's Messenger and Abu Bakr with white clothes to wear. When the Muslims of Medina heard the new of the departure of Allah's Messenger from Mecca (towards Medina), they started going to the Harra every morning,. They would wait for him till the heat of the noon forced them to return. One day, after waiting for a long while, they returned home, and when they went into their houses, a Jew climbed up to the roof of one of the forts of his people to look for something, and he saw Allah's Messenger and his companions, dressed in white clothes, emerging out of the desert mirage.

"The Jew could not help shouting at the top of his voice: 'O you Arabs! Here is your great man whom you have been waiting for!' So all the Muslims rushed to their arms and received Allah's Messenger on the summit of Harra. The Prophet turned with them to the right and alighted at the quarters of Bani Amr Ibn Auf, and this was on Monday in the month of Rabi ul Awal. Abu Bakr stood up, receiving the people, while Allah's Messenger sat down and kept silent. Some of the Ansar who came and had not seen Allah's Messenger before began greeting Abu Bakr, but when the sunshine fell on Allah's Messenger and Abu Bakr came forward and shaded him with his sheet, only then the people came to know Allah's Messenger. Allah's Messenger stayed with Bani Amr Ibn Auf for ten nights and established the mosque (Mosque of Quba) which was founded on piety. Allah's Messenger prayed in it and then mounted his she-camel and proceeded on, accompanied by the people till his she-camel knelt down at the place of the Mosque of Allah's Messenger at Medina. Some Muslims used to pray there in those days, and that place was a yard for drying dates belonging to Suhail and Sahl, the orphan boys who were under the guardianship of Asad In Zurara. When his she-camel knelt down, Allah's Messenger said: 'This place, Allah willing, will be our abiding place.' Allah's Messenger then called the two boys and told them to suggest a price for that yard so that he might take it as a mosque. The two boys said: 'No, but we will give it as a gift, O Allah's Messenger!' Allah's Messenger then built a mosque there. The Prophet himself started carrying unburned bricks for its building and while doing so, he was saying: 'This load is better than the load of Khaibar, for it is more pious in the Sight of Allah and purer and better rewardable.' He was also saying: 'O Allah! The actual reward is the reward in the Hereafter, so bestow Your Mercy on the Ansar and the Emigrants.' Thus the Prophet recited (by way of proverb) the poem of some Muslim poet whose name is unknown to me." (Ibn Shibab said, 'In the hadiths, it does not occur that Allah's Messenger recited a complete poetic verse other than this one.') (Sahih Al-Bukhari)

Thus was accomplished the hijrah, or the flight of Muhammad as called in European annals, from which the Islamic calendar dates.

When the Prophet Muhammad and his companions settled at Yathrib, this city changed its name, and henceforth was called, Al-Medina, Al-Munawara, the Illuminated City, or more shortly, Medina, the City. It is situated about eleven-day's journey to the north of Mecca. At that time it was ruled by two Kahtanite tribes, Aws and Khazraj. These two tribes, however, were constantly quarreling among themselves. It was only about that time when the Prophet announced his mission at Mecca that these tribes, after long years of continuous warfare, entered on a period of comparative peace. When the Prophet settled at Medina, the tribes of Aws and Khazraj forgot entirely their old feuds and were united together in the bond of Islam. Their old divisions were soon effaced and the Ansar", the Helpers of the Prophet, became the common designation of all Medinites who had helped the Prophet in his cause. Those who emigrated with him from Mecca received the title of "Muhajereen" or the Emigrants. The Prophet, in order to unite both classes in closer bonds, established between them a brotherhood, which linked them together as children of the same parents, with the Prophet as their guardian.

The first step the Prophet took, after his settlement at Medina, was to built a mosque for the worship of Allah according to principles of Islam. Also, houses for the accommodation of the emigrants were soon erected.

Medina and its suburb were at this time inhabited by three distinct parties, the Emigrants, the Helpers, and the Jews. In order to weld them together into an orderly federation, the Prophet granted a charter to the people, clearly defining their rights and obligations. This charter represented the framework of the first commonwealth organized by the Prophet. It started thus: 'In the name of he Most Merciful and Compassionate Lord, this charter is given by Muhammad, the Messenger of Allah to all believers, whether of Quraish or Medina, and all individuals of whatever origin who have made common cause with them, who shall all constitute one nation."

The following are some extracts from the charter: The state of peace and war shall be common to all Muslims; no one among them shall have the right of concluding peace with, or declaring war against, the enemies of his co-religionists. The Jews who attach themselves to our commonwealth shall be protected from all insults and vexations; they shall have an equal right with our people to our assistance and good offices. The Jews of the various branches and all others doiciled in Medina shall form with the Muslims one composite nation; they shall practice their religion as freely as the Muslims. The allies of the Jews shall enjoy the same security and freedom. The guilty shall be pursued and punished. The Jews shall join the Muslims in defending Medina all enemies. The interior of Medina shall be a sacred place for all who accept this charter. All true Muslims shall hold in abhorrence every man guilty of crime, injustice or disorder; no one shall uphold the culpable, though he be his nearest kin.

After dealing with the interior management of the State, the charter concluded as follows: "All future disputes arising among those who accept this charter shall be referred, under Allah to the Prophet."

Thus this charter put an end to the state of anarchy that prevailed among the Arabs. It constituted the Prophet Muhammad as chief magistrate of the nation.

The party of the Ansars, or Helpers, included some lukewarm converts who retained an ill-concealed predilection for idolatry. These were headed by Abdullah Ibn Ubai, a man with some claims to distinction. They ostensibly joined Islam, but in secret were disaffected. They often were a source of considerable danger to the newborn commonwealth and required unceasing watchfulness on the part of the Prophet. Towards them he always showed the greatest patience and forbearance, hoping in the end to win them over to the faith, which expectations were fully justified by the result. While the death of

Abdullah Ibn Ubai, his party which were known as the party of the "Munafiqeen" (the Hypocrites) disappeared.

The Jews who constituted the third party of the Medinites were, however, the most serious element of danger. No kindness or generous treatment on the part of the Prophet would seem to satisfy them. They soon broke off and ranged themselves with the enemies of the new faith. They did not hesitate to declare openly that they preferred idolatry, with its attendant evils, to the faith of Islam. Thus, the Prophet had to keep an eye on his enemies outside Medina, on the one hand, and those within the city on the other. The Meccans who had sworn Muhammad's death were well acquainted, thanks to the party of the Hypocrites and of the Jews at Medina, with the real forces of the Muslims. They also knew that the Jews had accepted Muhammad's alliance only from motives of temporary expedience and that they would break away from him to join the idolaters as soon as the latter showed themselves in the vicinity of Medina. The safety of the state required the proscription of the traitors who were secretly giving information to the common enemy. About six men were executed for high treason of this nature.

Towards the second year of the hijrah, the idolaters of Mecca began a series of hostile acts against the Muslims of Medina. They sent men in parties to commit depredations on the fruit trees of the Muslims of Medina and to carry away their flocks. Now came the moment of severest trial to Islam. It became the duty of the Prophet to take serious measures to guard against any plot rising from within or a sudden attack from without. He put Medina in a state of military discipline. He had to send frequent reconnoitering parties to guard against any sudden onslaught. No sooner did the Prophet organize hi state than a large well-equipped army of the Meccans was afield. A force constituting of one thousand men marched under Abu Jahl, a great enemy of Islam, towards Medina to attack the city. The Muslims received timely notice of their enemies' intention. A body of three hundred adherents, of whom two thirds were citizens of Medina, was gathered to forestall the idolaters by occupying the valley of Badr, situated near the sea between Mecca and Medina. When the Prophet saw the army of the infidels approaching the valley, he prayed that the little band of Muslims might not be destroyed.

The army of the Meccans advanced into the open space which separated the Muslims from the idolaters. According to Arab usage, the battle was began by simple combats. The engagement that became general. The result of the battle was that the Meccans were driven back with great loss. Several of their chiefs were slain, including Abu Jahl. A large number of idolaters remained prisoners in the hands of the Muslims. They were, contrary to all usage and traditions of the Arabs, treated with the greatest humanity. The Prophet gave strict orders that sympathy should be shown to them in their misfortune and that they should be treated with kindness. These instructions were faithfully obeyed by the Muslims to whose care the prisoners were confided. Dealing with this event, Sir William Muir, in his book Life of Muhammad, quotes one of the prisoners saying: "Blessing be on the men of Medina; they made us ride, while they themselves walked; they gave us wheaten bread to eat, when there was little of it, contenting themselves with dates."

Almighty Allah said: *And Allah has already made you victorious at Badr, when you were a weak little force. So fear Allah much (abstain from all kinds of sins and evil deeds which He has forbidden and love Allah much, perform all kinds of good deeds which He has ordained) that you may be grateful. (Remember) when you (Muhammad) said to the believers, "is it not enough for you that your Lord (Allah) should help you with three thousand angels; sent down? Yes, if you hold on to patience and piety, and the enemy comes rushing at you; your Lord will help you with five thousand angels having marks of distinction. Allah made it not but as a message of good news for you and as an assurance to your hearts. And there is no victory except from Allah the All Mighty, the All Wise. That He might cut off a part of those who disbelieve, or expose them to infamy, so that they retire frustrated." (Ch 3:123-127 Quran).*

The remarkable circumstances, which led to the victory of Badr, and results, which followed from it, made a deep impression on the minds of the Muslims; the angels of the heaven had battled on their side against their enemies. The division of the spoils created some dissension between the Muslim warriors. For the moment, the Prophet divided it equally among all. Subsequently, a Qur'an revelation laid down a rule for future division of the spoils. According to this rule, a fifth was reserved for the public treasury for the support of the poor and indigent, while the distribution of the remaining four fifths was left to the discretion of the Chief of the State.

The next battle between the Quraish and the Muslims was the battle of Uhud, a hill about four miles to the north of Medina. The idolaters, to revenge their loss at Badr, made tremendous preparations for a new attack upon the Muslims. They collected an army of three thousand strong men, of whom seven hundred were armed with coats of mail, and two hundred horses. These forces advanced under the conduct of Abu Sufyan and encamped at a village six miles from Medina, where they gave themselves up to spoiling the fields and flocks of the Medinites. The Prophet, being much inferior to his enemies in number, at first determined to keep himself within the town and to receive them there; but afterwards, the advice of some of his companions prevailing he marched out against them at the head of one thousand men, of whom one hundred were armed with coats of mail; but he had no more than one horse, besides his own, in his whole army. With these forces he halted at Mount Uhud. He was soon abandoned by Abdullah Ibn Ubai, the leader of the Hypocrites, with three hundred of his followers. Thus, the small force of the Prophet was reduced to seven hundred.

At Mount Uhud the Muslim troops passed the night, and in the morning, after offering their prayers, they advanced into the plain. The Prophet contrived to have the hill at his back, and, the better to secure his men from being surrounded, he placed fifty archers on the height in the rear, behind the troops, and gave them strict orders not to leave their posts whatever might happen. When they came to engage, the Prophet had superiority at first. But afterward, his archers left their position for the sake of plunder, thus allowing the enemy to attack the Muslims in the fear and surround them. The Prophet lost the day and very nearly lost his life. He was struck down by a shower of stones and wounded in the face by two arrows, and one of his front teeth was broken. Of the Muslims, seventy men were killed, among whom was the Prophet's uncle Hamza. Of the infidels, twenty-two men were lost.

The Quraish were too exhausted to follow up their advantage, either by attacking Medina or by driving the Muslims from the heights of Uhud. They retreated from the Medinite territories after barbarously mutilating the corpses of their dead enemies.

Almighty Allah said: *So do not become weak (against your enemy), nor be sad, and you will be superior (in victory) if you are indeed (true) believers. If a wound (and killing) has touched you, be sure a similar wound (and killing) has touched the others. And so are the days (good and not so good), We give to men by turns, that Allah may test those who believe, and that He may take martyrs from among you. And Allah likes not the Zalimeen (polytheists and wrongdoers).*

And that Allah may test (or purify) the believers (from sins) and destroy the disbeliveers. Do you think that you will enter Paradise before Allah tests those of you who fought (in His Cause) and (also) tests those who are patient? You did indeed wish for death (Ash-shahadah- martyrdom) before you met it. Now you have seen it openly with your own eyes." (Ch 3:139-143 Quran)

Allah the Exalted also said: We shall cast terror into the hearts of those who disbelieve, because they joined others in worship with Allah for which He has sent no authority; their abode will be the Fire and how evil is the abode of the Zalimeen (polytheists and wrong-doers). And Allah did indeed fulfil His Promise to you when you were killing them (your enemy) with His Permission; until (the moment) you lost your courage and fell to disputing about the order, and disobeyed after He showed you (of the booty) which you love. Among you are some that desire this world and some that desire the Hereafter. Then He made you flee from them (your enemy), and

He might test you. But surely, He forgave you, and Allah is most Gracious to the believers.

And remember when you ran away (dreadfully) without even a casting a side-glance at anyone, and the Messenger (Muhammad) was in your rear calling you back. There did Allah give you one distress after another by way of requital to teach you not to grieve for that which had escaped you, nor that which had befallen you. And Allah is Well Aware of all that you do.

Then after the distress, He sent down security for you. Slumber overtook a party of you, while another party was thinking about themselves (as how to save their ownselves, ignoring the others and the Prophet) and thought wrongly of Allah - the thought of ignorance. They said, "Have we any part in the affair?" Say you (O Muhammad): "Indeed the affair belongs wholly to Allah." They hide within themselves what they dare not reveal to you, saying: "If we had anything to do with the affair, none of us would have been killed here." Say: "Even if you had remained in your homes, those for whom death was decreed would certainly have gone forth to the place of their death," but that Allah might test what is in your breasts; and to Mahis (to test, to purify, to get rid of) that which was in your hearts (sins), and Allah is All Knower of what is in (your) breasts." (Ch 3:151-154 Quran).

Narrated Al-Baraa' Ibn Azib: "The Prophet appointed Abdullah Ibn Jubair as the commander of the infantry men (archers) who were fifty on the day (of the battle) of Uhud. He instructed them: 'Stick to your place, and don't leave it even if you see birds snatching us, till I send for you; and if you see that we have defeated the infidels and made them flee, even then you should not leave your place till I send for you.' Then the infidels were defeated. By Allah I saw the women fleeing lifting up their clothes revealing their leg bangles and their legs. So, the companions of Abdullah Ibn Jubair said: "The booty! O people, the booty! Your companions have become victorious, what are you waiting for now?" Abdullah Ibn Jubair said: "Have you forgotten what Allah's Messenger said to you?" They replied: "By Allah! We will go to the people (the enemy) and collect our share from the war booty." But when they went to them, they were forced to turn back defeated. At that time Allah's Messenger in their rear was calling them back. Only twelve men remained with the Prophet, and the infidels martyred seventy men from us.

"The Prophet and his companions caused the Pagans to lose one hundred and forty men, seventy of whom were captured and seventy were killed. Then Abu Sufyan asked three times: 'Is Muhammad present among these people?' The Prophet ordered his companions not to answer him. Then he asked three times: 'Is Ibn Abu Quhafa present amongst these people?' He asked again three times: 'Is Ibn Al Khattab present among these people?' He then returned to his companions and said: 'As for these (men), they have been killed.' 'Umar could not control himself and said to Abu Sufyan: ' You told a lie, by Allah! O enemy of Allah! All those you have mentioned are alive, and the thing which will make you unhappy is still there.' Abu Sufyan said: 'Our victory today compensates for yours in the Battle of Badr, and in war (the victory) is always undecided and is shared in turns by the belligerents. You will find some of your killed men mutilated, but I did not urge my men to do so, yet I do not feel sorry for their deed.' After that he started reciting cheerfully: 'O Hubal, be superior!' On that the Prophet said (to his companions): 'Why don't you answer hiback?' They said: 'O Allah's Messenger! What shall we say?' He said: 'Say, Allah is Higher and more Sublime.' Then Abu Sufyan said: 'We have the idol of Al-Uzza, and you have no 'Uzza.' The Prophet said (to his companions): 'Why don't you answer him back?' They asked: 'O Allah's Messenger! What shall we say?' He said: 'Say Allah is our Helper and you have no helper.'" (Sahih Al Bukhari)

The moral effect of this disastrous battle was such as to encourage some neighboring nomad tribes to make forays upon the Medinte territories, but most of these were repelled.

The Jews also were not slow to involve in trouble the Prophet and his followers. They tried to create disaffection among his people and slandered him and his adherents. They mispronounced the words of the Qur'an so as to give them an offensive meaning. They also caused their poets, who were superior in culture and intelligence, to use their influence to sow sedition among the Muslims. One of their distinguished poets, called Ka'b, of the Bani An-Nadir, spared no efforts in publicly deploring the ill success of the idolaters after their defect at Badr.

By his satires against the Prophet and his disciples, and his elegies on the Meccans who had fallen at Badr, Ka'b succeeded in exciting the Quraish to that frenzy of vengeance which broke out at Uhud. He then returned to Medina, where he continued to attack the Prophet and the Muslims, men and women, in terms of the most obscene character. Though he belonged to the tribe of Bani An Nadir, which had entered into the compact with the Muslims and pledged itself both for the internal and external safety of the State, he openly directed his acts against the commonwealth of which he was a member.

Another Jew, Sallam by name, of the same tribe, behaved equally fiercely and bitterly against the Muslims. He lived with a party of his tribe at Khaibar, a village five days' journey northwest of Medina. He made every effort to excite the neighboring Arab tribes against the Muslims. The Muslim commonwealth with the object of securing safety among the community, passed a sentence of outlawry upon Ka'b and Sallam.

The members of another Jewish tribe, namely Bani Qainuqa', were sentenced to expulsion from the Medinite territory for having openly and knowingly infringed the terms of the compact. It was necessary to put an end to their hostile actions of the sake of maintaining peace and security. The Prophet had to go to their headquarters, where he required them to enter definitively into the Muslim commonwealth by embracing Islam or to leave Medina. To this they replied in the most offensive terms: "You have had a quarrel with men ignorant of the art of war. If you are desirous of having any dealings with us, we shall show you that we are men." They then shut themselves up in their fortress and set the Prophet and his authority at defiance. The Muslims decided to reduce them and laid siege to their fortress without loss of time. After fifteen days they surrendered. Though the Muslims at first intended to inflict some severe punishment on them, they contented themselves by banishing the Bani Qainuqa'.

The Bani An-Nadir had now behaved in the same way as Bani Qainuqa'. The had likewise, knowingly and publicly, disregarded the terms of the Charter. The Prophet sent them a message similar to that which was sent to their brethren, the Qainuqa'. Then, relying on the assistance of the Hypocrites' party, returned for a defiant reply. After a siege of fifteen days, they sued for terms. The Muslims renewed their previous offer, and the Jews of An Nadir chose to execute Medina. They were allowed to take with them all their movable property, with the exception of their arms. Before leaving Medina, they destroyed all their dwellings in immovable property and arms which they could not carry away with them were distributed by the Prophet with the consent of the Ansar and the Emigrants. A principle was henceforth adopted that any acquisition not made in actual warfare should belong to that state and that its disposal should be left to the discretion of the ruling authorities.

Almighty Allah said: *(And there is also a share in this booty) for the poor emigrants, who were expelled from their homes and their property, seeking Bounties from Allah and to please Him. And helping Allah (helping His Religion) and His Messenger (Muhammad). Such are indeed the truthful (to what we say); and those who, before them, had homes (in Al Madina) and had adopted the Faith, love, those who emigrate to them, and have no jealousy in their breasts for that which they have been given (from the booty of Bani An Nadir), and give them (emigrants) preference over themselves, even though they were in need of that. And whosoever is saved from his own covetousness, such are they who will be the successful." (Ch 59:8-9 Quran)*

The expulsion of the Bani An-Nadir took place in the fourth year of the hijrah. The remaining portion of this year and the early part of the next were passed in repressing the hostile attempts of the nomadic tribes against the Muslims and inflicting punishment for various murderous forays on the Medinite territories. Of this nature was the expedition against the Christian Arabs of Dumat Al Jandal (a place about seven days' journey to the south of Damascus), who had stopped the Medinites traffic with Syria and even threatened a raid upon Medina. These marauders, however, fled on the approach of the Muslims, and the Prophet returned to Medina after concluding a treaty with a neighboring chief, to whom he granted permission of pasturage in the Medinite territories.

In the same year, the enemies of Islam made every possible attempt to stir up the tribes against the Muslims. The Jews also took an active, if hidden, part in those intrigues. An army of ten thousand well-equipped men, marched towards Medina under the command of Abu Sufyan. They encamped near Mount Uhud, a few miles from the city. The Muslims could gather only an army of three thousand men. Seeing their inferiority in numbers on the one hand, and the turbulence of the Hypocrites within the town on the other, they preferred to remain on the defensive. They dug a deep moat round the unprotected quarters of Medina and encamped outside the city with a trench in front of them. They relied for safety of the other side upon their allies, the Quaraiza, who possessed several fortresses at a short distance towards the south and were bound by the compact to assist the Muslim s against any raiders. These Jews, however, were induced by the idolaters to violate their pledge and to join the Quraish. As these Jews were acquainted with the Hypocrites within the walls of the city were waiting for an opportunity to play their part, the situation of the Muslims was most dangerous.

The siege had already lasted for twenty days. The enemy made great efforts to cross the trench, but every attempt was fiercely repulsed by the small Muslim force. Disunion was now rife in the midst of the besieging army. Their horses were perishing fast, and provisions were becoming less every day. During the night, a storm of wind and rain caused their tents to be overthrown and their lights extinguished. Abu Sufyan and the majority of his army fled, and the rest took refuge with the Quraiza. The Muslims, though they were satisfied with the failure of their enemies, could not help thinking that the victory was unsatisfactory so long as the Quraiza, who had violated their sworn pledge, remained so near. The Jews might at any time surprise Medina from their side. The Muslims felt it their duty to demand an explanation of the violation of the pledge. This was utterly refused. Consequently, the Jews were besieged and compelled to surrender at discretion. They only asked that their punishment should be left to the judgment of Sa'd Ibn Mu'adh, the prince of the tribe of Aws. This chief, who was a fierce soldier, had been wounded in the attack, and, indeed, died of his wounds the following day. Infuriated by the treacherous conduct of the Bani Quraiza, he gave judgment that the fighting men should be to death and that the women and children should become the slaves of the Muslims. The sentence was carried into execution.

It was about this time that the Prophet granted tot he monks of the Monastry of St. Catherine, near Mount Sinai, his liberal charter by which they secured for the Christians noble and generous privileges and immunities. He undertook himself and enjoined his followers, to protect the Christians, to defend their churches and the residences of their priests and to guard them from all injuries. They were not to be unfairly taxed; no bishop was to be driven out of his diocese; nor Christian was to be forced to reject his religion; no monk was to be expelled from his Monastry; no pilgrim was to be stopped from his pilgrimage; nor were the Christian churches to be pulled down for the sake of building mosques or houses for the Muslims. Christian women married to Muslims were to enjoy their own religion and not to be subjected to compulsion or annoyance of any kind. If the Christians should stand in need of assistance for the repair of their churches or monasteries, or any other matter pertaining to their religion, the Muslims were to assist them. This was not to be considered as supporting their religion, but as simply rendering them assistance in special circumstances. Should the Muslims be engaged in hostilities with outside Christians, no Christian resident among the Muslims should be treated with contempt on account of his creed. The Prophet declared that any Muslim violating any clause of the charter should be regarded as a transgressor of Allah's commandments, a violator of His testament and neglectful of His faith.

Six years had already elapsed since the Prophet and his Meccan followers had fled from their birthplace. Their hearts began to yearn for their homes and for their Sacred House the Ka'ba. As the season of the pilgrimage approached, the Prophet announced his intention to visit the holy center, and numerous voices of his disciples responded to the call. Preparations were soon made for the journey to Mecca. The Prophet, accompanied by seven or eight hundred Muslims, Emigrants and Ansars, all totally unarmed, set out on the pilgrimage. The Quraish, who were still full of animosity towards the Muslims, gathered a large army to prevent them from entering Mecca and maltreated the envoy whom the Prophet had sent to ask permission to visit the holy places. After much difficulty, a treaty was concluded by which it was agreed that all hostilities should cease for ten years; that anyone coming from the Quraish to the Prophet without the permission of the guardian or chief should be given back to the idolaters; that any Muslim persons going over to the Meccans should not be surrendered; that any tribe desirous of entering into alliance, either with the Quraish or with the Muslims, should be at liberty to do so without disputes; that the Muslims should go back to Medina on the present occasion and stop advancing further; that they should be permitted in the following year to visit Mecca and to remain there for three days with the arms they used on journeys, namely, their scimitars in sheaths.

The Treaty of Hudaibiya thus ended, the Prophet returned with his people to Medina.

About this time it was revealed to the Prophet that his mission should be universal. He dispatched several envoys to invite the neighboring sovereigns to Islam. The embassy to the king of Persia, Chosroes Parvis, was received with disdain and contumely. He was haughtily amazed at the boldness of the Mecca fugitive in addressing him on terms of equality. He was so enraged that he tore up into pieces the Prophet's letter of invitation to Islam and dismissed the envoy from his presence with great contempt. When the Prophet received information on this treatment, he calmly observed: "Thus will the Empire of Chosroes be torn to pieces."

The embassy to Heraclitus, the Emperor of the Romans, was received much more politely and reverentially. He treated the ambassador with great respect and sent the Prophet a gracious reply to his message.

Another envoy was sent to an Arab price of the Ghassanite tribe, a Christian feudatory of Heraclius. This prince, instead of receiving the envoy with any respect, cruelly murdered him. This act caused great consternation among the Muslims, who considered it as an outrage of international obligations.

Narrated Abdullah Ibn Abbas: Abu Sufyan Ibn Harb informed me that Heraclius had sent a messenger to him while he had been accompanying a caravan from Quraish. They were merchants doing business in Sham (Syria, Palestine, Lebanon, and Jordan) at the time when Allah's Messenger had a truce with Abu Sufyan and Quraish infidels. So Abu Sufyan and his companions went to Heraclius at Ilya (Jerusalem).

Heraclitus called them in the court and he had all the senior Roman dignitaries around him. He called for his translator who, translating Heraclius's question, said to them: "Who among you is closely related to that man who claims to be a Prophet?" Abu Sufyan replied: "I am the nearest relative to him (amongst the group)."

Heraclius said: "Bring him (Abu Sufyan) close to me and make his companions stand behind him." Abu Sufyan added: "Heraclius told his translator to tell my companions that he wanted to put some questions to me regarding that man (The Prophet) and if I told a lie they (my companions) should contradict me. By Allah! Had I not been afraid of my companions labeling me a liar, I would have not have spoken the truth about the Prophet." Abu Sufyan's narration continues:

"The first question he asked me about him was;

What is his family status among you?"

"I replied: "He belongs to a good noble family amongst us."

Heraclius further asked: "Has anybody among you ever claimed the same (to be a Prophet) before him?"

I replied: "No."

He said: "Was anybody amongst his ancestors a king?"

I replied: "No."

Heraclius asked: "Do the nobles or the poor follow him?"

I replied: "It is the poor who follow him."

He said: "Are his followers increasing or decreasing (day by day)?"

I replied: "They are increasing."

He then asked: "Does anybody amongst those who embrace his religion become displeased and renounce the religion afterwards?"

I replied: "No."

Heraclius said: "Have you ever accused him of telling lies before his claim (to be a Prophet)?"

I replied: "No."

Hereaclius said: "Does he break his promises?"

I replied: "No. We are at truce with him but we do not know what he will do in it." I could not find opportunity to say anything against him except that.

Heraclius asked: "Have you ever had a war with him?"

I replied: "Yes."

Then he said: "What was the outcome of the battles?"

I replied: "Sometimes he was victorious and sometimes we."

Heraclius said: "What does he order you to do?"

I said: "He tells us to worship Allah and Allah alone and not to worship anything along with Him, and to renounce all that our ancestors had said. He orders us to pray, to speak the truth, to be chaste and to keep good relations with our kith and kin."

Heraclius asked the translator to convey to me the following: "I asked you about his family and your reply was that he belonged to a very noble family. In fact, all the Messengers come from noble families among their respective peoples. I questioned you whether anybody else among you claimed such a thing; your reply was in the negative. If the answer had been in the affirmative, I would have thought that this man was following the previous man's statement. Then I asked you whether anyone of his ancestors was a king. Your reply was in the negative, and if it had been in the affirmative, I would have thought that this man wanted to take back his ancestral kingdom. I further asked whether he was ever accused of telling lies before he said what he said and your reply was in the negative. So I wondered how a person who does not tell a lie about others could ever tell a lie about Allah. I then asked you whether the rich people followed him or the poor. You replied that it was the poor who followed him. And, in fact, all the

Messengers have been followed by this veryclass of people. Then I asked you whether his followers were increasing or decreasing. You replied that they were increasing, and, in fact, this is the way of true faith, till it is complete in all respects. I further asked you whether there was anybody, who, after embracing his religion, became displeased and discarded his religion. You reply was in the negative, and, in fact this is (the sign of) true faith, when its delight enters the hearts and mixes with them completely. I asked you whether he had ever betrayed. You replied in the negative, and likewise the Messengers never betray. Then I asked you what he ordered you to do. You replied that he ordered you to worship Allah and Allah alone and not to worship anything along with Him, and forbade you to worship idols, and ordered you to pray, to speak the truth and to be chaste. If what you have said is true, he will very soon occupy this place underneath my feet and I kne w it (from the scriptures) that he was going to appear but I did not know that he would be from you, and if I could reach him definitely, I would go immediately to meet him and if I were with him, I would certainly wash his feet."

Heraclius then asked for the letter addressed by Allah's Messenger which had been delivered by Dihya to the Governor of Busra, who forwarded it to Heraclius to read. The contents of the letter were as follows: "In the name of Allah, the Beneficent, the Merciful. (This letter is) from Muhammad, the slave of Allah and His Messenger to Heraclius the ruler of Byzantine. Peace be upon him who follows the right path. Furthermore, I invite you to Islam, and if you become a Muslim you will be safe, and Allah will double your reward, and if you reject this invitation of Islam, you will be committing a sin by misguiding your subjects.

And I recite to you Allah's Statement: SAY (O Muhammad): 'O People of the Scripture (Jews & Christians): Come to a word that is just between us and you, that we worship none but Allah, and that we associate no partners with Him and that none of us shall take others as lords besides Allah.' Then, if they turn away, say: 'Bear witness that we are Muslims.' "

Abu Sufyan then added: When Heraclius had finished his speech and had read the letter, there was a great hue and cry in the Royal Court. So we turned out of the court. I told my companions that the question of Ibn-Abi-Kabsha (the Prophet Muhammad) had become so prominent that even the King of Bani Al-Asfar (Byzantine) was afraid of him. Then I started to become sure that he (the Prophet) would be the conqueror in the near future till I embraced Islam (Allah guided me to it).

The sub narrator added that Ibn An-Natur was the Governor of Ilya (Jerusalem) and Heraclius was the head of the Christians of Sham. Ibn An-Natur narrated that once while Heraclius was visiting Ilya (Jerusalem), he got up in the morning with a sad mood. Some of his priests asked him why he as in that mood. Hreaclius was a foreteller and an astrologer. He replied: "At night when I looked at the stars, I saw that the leader of those who practice circumcision had appeared (become the conqueror). Who are they who practice circumcision?" The people replied: "Except the Jews, nobody practices circumcision, so you should not be afraid of them (Jews). Just Issue orders to kill very Jew present in the country.'

While they were discussing it, a messenger sent by the king of Ghassan to convey the news of Allah's Messenger to Heraclius was brought in. Having heard the news, he (Heraclius) ordered the people to go and see whether the messenger of Ghassan was circumcised. The people, after seeing him, told Heraclius that he was circumcised. Heraclius then asked him about the Arabs. The messenger replied: "Arabs also practice circumcision."

After hearing that Heraclius remarked that sovereignty of the Arabs had appeared. Heraclius then wrote a letter to his friend in Rome who was as good as Heraclius in knowledge. Heraclius then left for Homs (a town in Syria) and stayed there till he received the reply of his letter from his friend, who agreed with him in his opinion about the emergence of the Prophet and the fact that he was a Prophet. On that, Heraclius invited all the heads of the Byzantines to assemble in his palace at Homs. When they assembled, he ordered that all the doors of his palace be closed. Then he came out and said: "O Byzantines! If success is your desire and if you seek right guidance and want your empire to remain, then give a pledge of allegiance to this Prophet (embrace Islam)."

(on hearing the views of Heraclius) the people ran towards the gates of the palace like onagers but found the doors closed. Heraclius realized their hatred towards Islam and when he lost the hope of their embracing Islam, he ordered that they should be brought back in audience.

(When they returned) he said: "What was already said was just to test the strength of your conviction and I have seen it." The people prostrated before him and became pleased with him, and this was the end of Heraclius's story (in connection with his faith). (Sahih Al-Bukhari)

In the same year the Jews of Khaibar, a strongly fortified territory at a distance of four days' journey from Medina, showed implacable hatred towards the Muslims. United by alliance with the tribe of Ghatfan, as well as with other cognate tribes, the Jews of Khaibar made serious attempts to for ma coalition against the Muslims. The Prophet and his adherents were apprised of this movement and immediate measures were taken in order to repress any new attack upon Medina. An expedition of fourteen hundred men was soon prepared to march against Khaibar. The allies of the Jews left them to face the war with the Muslims all alone. The Jews firmly resisted the attacks of the Muslims, but eventually all their fortress had to be surrendered, one after the other to their enemies. They prayed for forgiveness, which was accorded to them on certain conditions. Their lands and immovable property were secured to them, together with the free practice of their religion. After subduing Khaibar, the Muslims returned to Medina in safety.

Before the end of the year, it being the seventh year of the hijrah, the Prophet and his adherents availed themselves of their armistice with the Quraish to visit the holy Ka'ba. The Prophet, accompanied by two hundred Muslims, went to Mecca to perform the rites of pilgrimage. On this occasion the Quraish evacuated the city during the three days which the ceremonies lasted.

Sir William Muir, in his book, Life of Mohammed Vol. III comments on the incident as follows:

It was surely a strange sight, which at this time presented itself at the vale of Mecca, a sight unique in the history of the world. The ancient city is for three days evacuated by all its inhabitants, high and low, every house deserted, and as they retire, the exiled converts, many years banished from their birth-place, approach in a great body accompanied by their allies, revisit the empty homes of their childhood, and within the short allotted space, fulfil the rites of pilgrimage. The outside inhabitants, climbing the heights around take refuge under tents or other shelter among the hills and glens; and clustering on the overhanging peak of Abu Qubeis, thence watch the movements of the visitors beneath, as with the Prophet at their head, they make the circuit of the Ka'ba and rapid procession between Essafa and Marwah, and anxiously scan every figure, if perchance they may recognize among the worshippers some long lost friend or relative. It was a scene rendered only by the throes, which gave birth to Islam.

In accordance with the terms of the treaty, the Muslims left Mecca at the end of three day's visit. This peaceful visit was followed by important conversions among the Quraish. Khalid Ibn Al-Walid, known as the Sword of Allah, who, before this, had been a bitter enemy of Islam and who commanded the Quraish cavalry at Uhud; and Amr Ibn Al' As, another important character and warrior, adopted the new faith.

When the Prophet and his followers returned to Medina, they arranged in expedition to exact retribution from the Ghassanite prince who had killed the Muslim envoy. A force of three thousand men, under the Prophet's adopted son Zaid, was sent to take reparation from the offending tribe.

Khalid Ibn Al-Walid was one of the generals chosen for the expedition. When they reached the neighborhood of Muta, a village to the southeast of the Dead Sea, they met with an overwhelming force of Arabs and Romans who were assembled to oppose them. The Muslims, however, resolved resolutely to push forward. Their courage was of no avail and they suffered great losses. In this battle Zaid and Ja'far, a cousin of the Prophet, and several other notables were killed. Khalid Ibn Al-Walid, by a series of maneuvers, succeeded in drawing off the army and conducting it without further loses to Medina. A month later, however, Amr Ibn Al-' As marched unopposed through the lands of the hostile tribes, received their submission, and restored the prestige of Islam on the Syrian frontier.

About the end of the seventh year of the hijrah, the Quraish and their allies, the Bani Bakr, violated the terms of the peace concluded at Hudaibiya by attacking the Bani Khuzaah, who were in alliance with the Muslims. The Bani Khuzzah appealed to the Prophet for help and protection. The Prophet determined to make a stop to the reign of injustice and oppression, which had lasted so long at Mecca. He immediately gathered ten thousand men to march against the idolaters and set out on January, 630.

After eight days the Muslims army halted, and alighted at Marr Az-Zahran, a day's journey from Mecca. On the night of their arrival, Abu Sufyan, who was delegated by the Quraish to ask the Prophet to abandon his project, presented himself and besought an interview. In the morning it was granted. "Has the time not come, O Abu Sufyan," said the Prophet, "for you to acknowledge that there is no deity save Allah and that I am His Messenger?" Abu Sufyan, after hesitating for awhile, pronounced the prescribed formula of belief and adopted Islam. He was then sent back to prepare the city for the Prophet's approach.

With the exception of a slight resistance by certain clans headed by Ikrima and Safwan, in which many Muslims were killed, the Prophet entered Mecca almost unopposed. The city which had treated him so cruelly, driven him and his faithful band for refuge among strangers, the city which had sworn his life and the lives of his devoted adherents, now lay at his mercy. His old persecutors were now completely at his feet. The Prophet entered Mecca on his favorite camel Al Kaswa, having Usama Ibn Zaid sitting behind him. On his way he recited Surah Al Fath (Victory), the first verses of which maybe interpreted thus: *Verily! We have given you (O Muhammad) a manifest victory. That Allah may forgive you your sins of the past and future, and complete His Favor on you, and guide you on the Straight Path; and that Allah may help you with strong help. (Ch 48:1-3 Quran)*

The Muslim army entered the city unpretentiously and peacefully. No house was robbed, no man or woman was insulted. The Prophet granted a general amnesty to the entire population of Mecca. Only four criminals, whom justice condemned, were proscribed. He did however, order the destruction of all idols and pagan images of worship, upon which three hundred and fifty idols which were in the Sacred House of Ka'ba were thrown down. The Prophet himself destroyed a wooden pigeon hung from the roof and regarded as one of the deities of the Quraish. During the downfall of the images and idols he was heard to cry aloud: "Allah is great. Truth has come and falsehood has vanished; verily falsehood is fleeting." The old idolaters observed thoughtfully the destruction of their gods, which were utterly powerless. After the Prophet had abolished these pagan idols and every pagan rite, he delivered a sermon to the assembled people. He dwelt upon the natural brotherhood of man in the words of the Qur'an: *O Mankind! We have created you for a male and a female, and made you into nations and tribes, that you may know one another. Verily, the most honorable of you in the Sight of Allah is that (believer) who has At-Taqwa (one of the Muttaqun, pious, and righteous persons who fear Allah much, abstain from all kinds of sins and evil deeds which He has forbidden), and love Allah much (perform all kinds of good deeds which He has ordained.) Verily Allah is All-Knowing, All-Aware. (Ch 49:13 Quran)*

Narrated Hisham's father: When Allah's Messenger set out (towards Mecca) during the year of the Conquest (of Mecca) and this news reached (the infidels of Quraish), Abu Sufyan, Hakim Ibn Hizam and Budail Ibn Waraqa came out to gather information about Allah's Messenger. They proceeded on their way till they reached a place called Marr-az-Zahran (which is near Mecca). Behold! There they saw many fires as if they were the fires of Arafat." Budail Ibn Waraqa' said: "Banu' Amr are less in number than that." Some of the guards of Allah's Messenger saw them and took them over, caught them, and bthem to Allah's Messenger. Abu Sufyan embraced Islam.

When the Prophet proceeded, he said to Al' Abbas: "Keep Abu Sufyan standing at the top of the mountain so that he would look at the Muslims. SO Al- Abbas kept him standing (at that place) and the tribes with the Prophet started passing in front of Abu Sufyan in military batches. A batch passed in front of Abu Sufyan and said: "O 'Abbas who are these?" 'Abbas said: "They are Banu Ghaifar." Abu Sufyan said: "I have got nothing to do with Ghifar." Then a batch of the tribe of Juhaina passed by and he said similarly as above. Then a batch of the tribe of Sa'd Ibn Huzaim passed by and he said similarly as above. Then came a batch, the like of which Abu Sufyan had not seen. He said: "Who are these?" Abbas said: "They are the Ansar headed by Sa'd Ibn 'Ubada, the one holding the flag." Sa'd Ibn 'Ubada said: "O Abu Sufyan! Today is the day of a great battle and today (what is prohibited in)the Ka'ba will be permissible." Abu Sufyan said, "O Abbas! How excellent the day of destruction is!" Then came another batch of warriors which was the smallest of all the batches, and in it there was Allah's Messenger and his companions, and the flag of the Prophet was carried by Az-Zubair Ibn Al-Awwam. When Allah's Messenger passed by Abu Sufyan, the latter said to the Prophet: "Do you know what Sa'd Ibn Ubada said?" The Prophet said: "What did he say?" Abu Sufyan said: "He said so-and-so." The Prophet said: "Sa'd told a lie, but today Allah will give superiority to the Ka'ba and today the Ka'ba will be covered with a cloth covering." Allah's Messenger ordered that his flag be fixed at Al-Hajun.

Narrated Urwa: Nafi' Ibn Jubair Ibn Mut'im said: "I heard Al-Abbas saying to Az-Zubair Ibn Al- Awwam, 'O Abu Abdullah! Did Allah's Messenger order you to fix the flag here?' "Allah's Messenger ordered Khalid Ibn Al-Walid to enter Mecca from its upper part from Kadaa' while the Prophet himself entered from Kudaa. Two men from the cavalry of Khalid Ibn Al-Walid named Hubaish Ibn Al Ashar and Kurz Ibn Jabir Al-Fihri were martyred on that day. (Sahih Al Bukhari)

Now great multitudes came to adopt Islam and take the oath of allegiance to the Prophet. For this purpose an assembly was held at As-Safa Mountain. Umar, acting as the Prophet's deputy administered the oath, whereby the people bound themselves not to adore any deity but Allah to obey the Prophet to abstain from theft, adultery, infanticide, lying and backbiting. Thus was fulfilled the prophecy embodied in the Surah Al Fath in the Quran.

During his stay at Mecca, the Prophet dispatched his principal disciples in every direction to preach Islam among the wild tribes of the desert and call them to the true religion of Allah. He sent small detachments of his troops into the suburbs who destroyed the temples of Al Uzza, Suwaa, and Manat, the three famous idols in the temples of the neighboring tribes. The Prophet gave strict orders that these expeditions should be carried out in a peaceable manner. These injunctions were obeyed in all cases, with one exception. The troops under Khalid Ibn Al-Walid, the fierce newly-converted warrior, killed a few of the Bani Jazima. When the news of this wanton bloodshed reached the Prophet, he was deeply grieved and exclaimed: "Oh, my Lord, I am innocent of what Khalid has done." He dispatched a large sum of money for the widows and orphans of the slain and severely rebuked Khalid.

At this time the tribes of Hawazin and Thakif showed unwillingness to render obedience to the Muslims without resistance. They formed a league with the intention of attacking the Prophet, but he was vigilant enough to frustrate their plan. A big battle was fought with this new enemy of Islam near Hunain, a deep and narrow defile nine miles northeast of Mecca. The idolaters were utterly defeated. One body of the enemy, consisting chiefly of the Thakif tribe, took refuge in their fortified city of Ta'if, which eight or nine years before had dismissed the Prophet from within its walls with injuries and insults. The remainder of the defeated force, consisting principally of the Hawazin, sought at a camp in the valley of Autas. This camp was raided by the Muslim troops. The families of the Hawazin, their flocks and herds with all their other effects, were captured by the troops of the Prophet. Ta'if was then besieged for a few days only, after which the Prophet raised the siege, well knowing that the people of Ta'if would soon be forced by circumstances to submit without bloodshed. Returning to his camp where the prisoners of Hawazin were left safely, the Prophet found a deputation from this hostile tribe who begged him to set free their families. The Prophet replied that he was willing to give back his own share of those captives and that of the children of Abdul Muttalib, but that he could not force his followers to abandon the fruits of their victory. The disciples followed the generous example of their teacher. The hearts of several members of the Thakir tribe were so influenced by this that they offered their allegiance and soon became earnest Muslims. The Prophet now returned to Medina fully satisfied with the achievements of his mission.

The ninth year of the hijrah is known as the Year of Embassies, as being the year in which the various tribes of Arabia submitted to the claim of the Prophet and sent embassies to render homage to him.

These tribes had been awaiting the issue of the war between Muhammad and the Quraish; but as soon as the tribe - the principal of the whole nation and the descendants of Ishmael, whose prerogatives none offered to dispute - had submitted, they were satisfied that it was not in their power to oppose Muhammad. Hence their embassies flocked into Medina to make their submission to him. The conquest of Mecca decided the fate of idolatry in Arabia. Now deputations began to arrive from all sides to render the adherence to Islam of various tribes. Among the rest, five princes of the tribe of Himyar professed Islam and sent ambassadors to notify Muhammad of the same. These were the princes of Yemen, Mahra, Oman, and Yamama.

The idolaters of Ta'if, the very people who had driven the Messenger of Islam from their midst with violence and contempt, now sent a deputation to pray forgiveness and ask to be numbered among his followers. They begged, however, for temporary preservation of their idols. As a last appeal they begged for one month of grace only. But even this was not conceded. The Prophet said Islam and the idols could not exist together. They then begged for exemption from the daily prayers. The Prophet replied that without devotion, religion would be nothing. At last they submitted to all that was required of them. They, however, asked to be exempted from destroying the idols with their own hands. This was granted. The Prophet selected Abu Sufyan and Mughira to destroy the idols of Ta'if, the chief of which was the notorious idol of Al-Lat. This was carried out amidst cries of despair and grief from the women of Ta'if.

The conversion of this tribe of Ta'if is worthy of notice. This tribe, which hither to had proved hostile to the new faith, was noted among the Arabs for its idolatrous priesthood. A small detachment under Ali was sent to reduce them to obedience and to destroy their idols. The prince of the tribe was 'Adi, the son of the famous Hatim, whose generosity was spoken of all over Arabia. On the approach of the Muslim force, Adi fled to Syria, leaving his sister with his principal clansmen, to fall into the hands of the Muslims. These were conducted by Ali with every sign of respect and sympathy to Medina. When the daughter of Hatim came before the Prophet, she addressed him in the following words: "Messenger of Allah, my father is dead; my brother, my only relation fled into the mountains on the approach of the Muslims. I cannot ransom myself; I count on your generosity for my deliverance. My father was an illustrious man, the prince of his tribe, a man who ransomed prisoners, protected the honor of women, fed the poor, cothe afflicted, and was deaf to no appeal." The Prophet replied: "Your father had the virtues of a true Muslim; if it were permitted to invoke the mercy of Allah on any whose life was passed in idolatry, I would pray to Allah for mercy for the soul of Hatim." Then, addressing the Muslims around him, he said: "the daughter of Hatim is free, her father was a generous and humane man; Allah loves and rewards the merciful." With the daughter of Hatim, all her people were set at liberty. She proceeded to Syria and related to her brother the generosity of Muhammad. 'Adi, touched by gratitude, hastened to Medina, where he was kindly received by the Prophet. He professed

Islam and returned to his people and persuaded them to abandon idolatry. They all submitted and became devoted Muslims.

Hitherto no prohibition had been enforced against idolaters entering the Holy Ka'ba, or performing their abominable rites within the sacred precincts. Towards the end of the ninth year of the hijrah, during the month of pilgrimage 'Ali was delegated by the Prophet to read a proclamation that ran as follows: "No idolater shall after this year perform the pilgrimage; no one shall make the circuit of the Ka'ba naked (such a disgraceful custom was practiced by the pagan Arabs); and treaty with the Prophet shall continue in force but four months are allowed to every man to return to his territories; after that there will be no obligation on the Prophet, except towards those with whom treaties have been concluded."

The vast multitude who had listened to the above declaration returned to their homes, and before the following year was over the majority of them were Muslims.

During the tenth year of the hijrah, as in the preceding one, numerous embassies continued to pour into Medina from all parts of Arabia, to testify to the allegiance of their chiefs and their tribes. Teachers were sent by the Prophet into the different provinces to teach the new converts the principles and precepts of Islam. These teachers were invariably given the following injunctions when they were about to depart on their mission: "Deal gently with the people, and be not harsh; cheer them, and do not look down upon them with contempt. You will meet with many believers in the Holy Scriptures, who will ask you: 'What is the key to heaven?' Answer them it (the key to heaven) is to bear witness to the divine truth and to do good."

Thus, the mission of the Prophet Muhammad was now accomplished; the whole work was achieved in his lifetime. Idolatry with its nameless abominations was entirely destroyed. The people who were sunk in superstition, cruelty, and vice in regions where spiritual life was utterly unknown were now united in one bond of faith, hope and charity. The tribes which had been from time immemorial engaged in perpetual wars were now united together by the ties of brotherhood, love, and harmony. Henceforth, their aims were not confined to this earth alone; but there was something beyond the grave - much higher, purer, and diviner - calling them to the practice of charity, goodness, justice, and universal love. They could now perceive that Allah was not that which they had carved out of wood or stone, but the Almighty Loving, Merciful, the Creator of the Universe.

On the return of the sacred month of pilgrimage, the Prophet, under the presentiment of his approaching end, determined to make a farewell pilgrimage to Mecca. In February 632, he left Medina with a very considerable concourse of Muslims. It is stated that from ninety thousand to one hundred and forty thousand people accompanied the Prophet. Before completing all rites of the pilgrimage, he addressed the assembled multitude from the top of Mount Arafat in the following words:

"O people! Listen to my words, for I know not whether another year will be vouchsafed to me after this year to find myself among you. Your lives and property are sacred and inviolable among one another until you appear before the Lord, as this day and this month are sacred for all; and remember, you will have to appear before your Lord Who will demand from you an account for all your actions. O people, you have rights over your wives, and your wives have a right over you. Verily you have taken them on the security of Allah and have made their people lawful unto you by the words of Allah. And your slaves, see that you feed them with such food as you eat yourselves, and clothe them with the stuff you wear, and if they commit a fault which you are not inclined to forgive, then part with them; for they are the servants of the Lord and are not to be harshly treated. O people, listen to my words and understand them. Know that all Muslims are brothers. You are one brotherhood; but no man shall take ought from his brother, unless by his free consent. Keep yourselves from injustice. Let him who is present tell this to him who is absent. It maybe that he who is told this afterward may remember better than he who has now heard it.

The Prophet concluded his sermon by exclaiming: "O Lord, I have fulfilled my message and accomplished my work." The assembled multitude, all in one voice, cried: "Yea, verily you have." The Prophet again exclaimed: "O Lord, I beseech You, bear witness to it."

Having rigorously performed all the ceremonies of the pilgrimage, that his example might be followed by all Muslims for all succeeding ages, the Prophet returned with his followers to Medina.

The eleventh year of the hijrah, being the last year of Muhammad's life, was spent at Medina. There he settled the organization of the provincial and tribal communities which had adopted Islam and become the component parts of the Muslims federation. More officers had to be deputed to the interior provinces for the purpose of teaching their inhabitants the precepts of the religion, administering justice, and collecting Zakat. Muadh Ibn Jabal was sent to Yemen. On his departure to that distant province the Prophet enjoined him to use his own discretion in the event of his being unable to find express authority in the Quran. Ali was deputed to Yamama in the southeast of the peninsula. To him the Prophet said: "Never decide between any two parties who come to you for justice unless you first hear both of them."

A force was not being prepared under Usama, Ibn Zaid, whose father was killed at Muta, against the Byzantines, to exact the long-delayed reparation for the murder of the envoy to Syria. However, the news of the Prophet's sickness and failing health caused that expedition to be stopped. This news was soon noised abroad and produced disorder in some districts. Three pretenders had arisen who gave themselves out as prophets and tried by all kinds of imposture to win over their tribes. The most dangerous of these pretenders was known as Al Aswad. He was a chief of Yemen and a conjurer. He soon succeeded in gaining over his tribesmen and, with the help, reduced to subjection many of the neighboring towns. He killed Shahr, whom the Prophet had appointed as Governor of Sana in the place of his father Bazan, who had just died. Bazan had been the viceroy of Yemen under Chosroes of Persia; after he had adopted Islam he was allowed by the Prophet to remain as Governor of Yemen. He was able to convert to Islam all the Persian colony in that province. Al-Aswad, the conjurer, had now killed Shahr, but soon after he was massacred by the Persians of Yemen.

The other two pretenders, Tulayha and Haroun by name, were not suppressed until after the death of the Prophet, during the reign of Abu Bakr. Haroun, better known as Mussaylamah, addressed to the Prophet a letter which ran as follows: "From Mussaylamah the Prophet of Allah, to Muhammad the Prophet of Allah. Peace be to you. I am your partner. Let the exercise of authority be divided between us. Half the earth will be mine, and half will belong to your Quraish. But the Quraish are too greedy to be satisfied with a just division." To this letter the Prophet replied as follows: "From Muhammad the Messenger of Allah to Mussaylamah the liar. Peace be to those who follow the right path. The earth belongs to Allah. It is He Who makes the reign whomsoever He pleases. Only those will prosper who fear the Lord."

The health of the Prophet grew worse. His last days were remarkable for the calmness and serenity of his mind. He was able, though weak and feeble, to lead the public prayers until within three days of his death. He requested that he might be permitted to stay at 'Aisha's house close to the mosque during his illness, an arrangement to which his other wives assented. As long as his strength lasted, he took part in the public prayers. The last time he appeared in the mosque he addressed the congregation, after the usual prayers were over, in the following words: "O Muslims, if I have wronged anyone of you, here I am to answer for it; if I owe anything to anyone, all I may happen to possess belongs to you." A man in the crowd rose and claimed three Dhirhams which he had given to a poor man at the request of the Prophet. They were immediately paid back with these words: "Better to blush in this world than in the next."

The Prophet then prayed and implored Allah's mercy for those who had fallen in the persecution of their enemies. He recommended to all his followers the observance of religious duties and the leading of a life of peace and goodwill. Then he spoke with emotion and with a voice still so powerful as to reach beyond the outer doors of the mosque: "By the Lord in Whose hand lies the soul of Muhammad as to myself, no man can lay hold on me in any matter; I have not made lawful anything excepting what Allah has made lawful; nor have I prohibited anything but that which Allah in His Book has prohibited."

Then turning to the women who sat close by, he exclaimed: "O Fatimah, my, daughter, and Safia, my aunt, work you both that which procure you acceptance with the Lord, for verily I have no power to save you in any wise." He then rose and re-entered the house of Aisha.

After this, the Prophet never appeared at public prayers. A few hours after he returned from the mosque, the Prophet died while laying his head on the bosom of Aisha. As soon as the Prophet's death was announced, a crowd of people gathered at the door of the house of Aisha, exclaiming: "How can our messenger be dead?" Umar said: "No, he is not dead; he will be restored to us, and those are traitors to the cause of Islam who say he is dead. If they say so let them be cut in pieces." But Abu Bakr entered the house at this moment, and after he had touched the body of the Prophet with a demonstration of profound affection, he appear at the door and addressed the crowd with the following speech: "O Muslims, if anyone of you has been worshipping Muhammad, then let me tell you that Muhammad is dead. But if you really do worship Allah then know that Allah is living and will never die. Do you forget the verse in the Quran: *Muhammad is not more than a Messenger, and indeed (many) Messengers have passed away before him. If he dies or is killed, will you then turn your back on your heels (as disbeliveers)? And he who turns back on his heels, not the least harm will he do to Allah, and Allah will give reward to those who are grateful." (Ch 3:144 Quran).* Upon hearing this speech of Abu Bakr, 'Umar acknowledged his error, and the crowd was satisfied and dispersed.

Al-Abbas, the Prophet's uncle, presided at the preparation for the burial, and the body was duly washed and perfumed. There was some dispute between the Quraish and the Ansars as to the place of burial; however, Abu Bakr settled the dispute by affirming that he had heard the Prophet say that a prophet should be buried at the very spot where he died. A grave was accordingly dug in the ground within the house of Aisha and under the bed on which the Prophet died. In this grave the body was buried, and the usual rites were performed by those who were present.

Thus ended the glorious life of that Prophet Muhammad SAW.

May the peace and blessings of Allah be upon him.